RUTH BURROWS

St. Teresa of Avila

Contents

1

Introduction: The Life and Legacy of St. Teresa of Avila

St. Teresa of Avila, born Teresa Sánchez de Cepeda y Ahumada in 1515, is one of the most prominent figures in the history of Catholic spirituality. As a mystic, reformer, and Doctor of the Church, her life's work has profoundly influenced Christian theology and the practice of contemplative prayer. St. Teresa lived during a time of great religious upheaval, marked by the Protestant Reformation and the Catholic Church's efforts to counter it through the Counter-Reformation. Her contributions to the Carmelite Order, her spiritual writings, and her experiences of mystical union with God have left an enduring legacy that continues to inspire believers and seekers today.

Early Life and Religious Calling

St. Teresa was born into a devout family in Gotarrendura, Ávila, Spain. Her upbringing was marked by a deep sense of faith, which was a characteristic of her family's devotion to the Church. From an early age, Teresa exhibited a strong desire for a life of holiness, often reading the lives of saints and imagining herself as a martyr for Christ. This early zeal, however, was tempered by the realities of life, and as she grew older, she found herself drawn to more worldly pursuits.

At the age of 20, Teresa entered the Carmelite convent of the Incarnation in Ávila, a decision that initially caused her inner turmoil. The life of the convent was not as rigorous as she had imagined, and she struggled with her spiritual discipline. For many years, she experienced a spiritual dryness and a sense of separation from God, a theme she would later explore in her writings. Despite these early challenges, Teresa persevered, and it was through these struggles that she deepened her relationship with God, leading to the profound mystical experiences for

2

which she is remembered.

Mystical Experiences and Reformation Efforts

Teresa's mystical experiences, which began in her early thirties, became a central part of her spiritual life. These included visions of Christ, experiences of levitation, and deep moments of contemplative prayer. Rather than being viewed as purely supernatural occurrences, Teresa's mystical experiences were deeply tied to her theological insights. She viewed these moments as God's way of drawing her closer, and they became the foundation for her spiritual teachings.

It was during this time that Teresa became increasingly disillusioned with the lax practices within the Carmelite convents. She felt a strong calling to reform the Order and return it to its original values of poverty, simplicity, and contemplative prayer. With the support of key figures in the Church, including St. John of the Cross, she founded the Discalced Carmelite Order, a movement that sought to embrace a stricter, more devout form of monastic life. The reforms were met with resistance from both within and outside the Carmelite community, yet Teresa's leadership and unwavering faith guided the Order to success. Her efforts culminated in the establishment of many new convents across Spain.

St. Teresa's Writings and Teachings

One of St. Teresa's most enduring legacies is her body of spiritual writings. Her major works, *The Interior Castle*, *The Way of Perfection*, and her autobiography *The Life of Teresa of Jesus*, are considered masterpieces of Christian mysticism. In these texts, Teresa outlines her experiences of prayer, her understanding of the soul's journey toward union with God, and practical advice for those seeking a deeper spiritual life.

In *The Interior Castle*, Teresa uses the metaphor of a castle with

3

many rooms to describe the stages of spiritual development. She emphasizes the importance of humility, self-knowledge, and the necessity of contemplative prayer in moving toward the innermost chamber, where one experiences the profound presence of God. This work, in particular, has been influential in shaping Christian contemplative traditions.

The Way of Perfection serves as a guide for her fellow nuns in living a life dedicated to prayer and self-sacrifice. It offers insights into Teresa's personal struggles and her deep reliance on God's grace in overcoming them. Her autobiography, *The Life of Teresa of Jesus*, provides a firsthand account of her spiritual journey, written not for her own glory, but to encourage others to trust in God's providence.

Legacy as a Doctor of the Church

St. Teresa of Avila was canonized in 1622, and in 1970, she was declared a Doctor of the Church by Pope Paul VI, making her the first woman to receive this title. This recognition underscores her importance not only as a mystic and reformer but also as a theologian whose insights into prayer and the spiritual life continue to resonate within the Church.

Her influence extends far beyond the Carmelite Order. St. Teresa's teachings on contemplative prayer have shaped the practices of religious communities worldwide, and her emphasis on the interior life continues to inspire individuals seeking a deeper connection with God. She remains a powerful symbol of spiritual fortitude, a woman who, in the face of personal struggles, institutional resistance, and physical illness, found strength in her faith and dedication to God.

2

Early Life and Family Background

St. Teresa of Avila, born as Teresa Sánchez de Cepeda y Ahumada, came into the world on March 28, 1515, in Gotarrendura, a small village near the city of Ávila, Spain. She was the third of nine children born to Alonso Sánchez de Cepeda and Beatriz de Ahumada. The circumstances of her early life, her family's religious dedication, and her formative experiences shaped the future saint's spiritual path, setting the foundation for her later works of reform and mysticism.

Family Heritage and Religious Influence

Teresa's family background played a significant role in her early development. Her father, Alonso Sánchez de Cepeda, was a devout Christian and a man of noble descent, with deep-rooted values in both religion and discipline. His commitment to the faith permeated the family's daily life, and Teresa later reflected on the strong moral code that her father instilled in her. Alonso was a widower when he married Teresa's mother, Beatriz, a woman of considerable virtue and piety who encouraged Teresa's early devotion to God. Beatriz, known for her kindness and faith, had a profound influence on Teresa, particularly in fostering her early love for reading devotional books, including the lives of saints.

Teresa's upbringing was steeped in Catholic tradition. The Spain of her childhood was a fervently religious country, still influenced by the Reconquista, which had ended a few decades before her birth. Catholicism was central to both public and private life, and this intense religious atmosphere shaped Teresa's worldview. Her family, though noble, was not immune to hardship. Her paternal grandfather had converted from Judaism to Christianity to avoid the persecution of Jews during the Spanish Inquisition, which left the family in a precarious

6

social position. This history of religious persecution, though not openly discussed, may have influenced Teresa's sense of spiritual resilience and her drive for reform.

Teresa's Early Devotion and Aspirations

From a young age, Teresa displayed a strong religious fervor. One of the most notable stories from her childhood is her attempt, at the age of seven, to run away from home with her brother, Rodrigo. The two siblings had been reading about the lives of saints and martyrs, and they set out with the goal of reaching Moorish lands to die as martyrs for their faith. Though their plan was thwarted by a family member who discovered them on the road, the incident highlights the intensity of Teresa's early spiritual aspirations.

Despite her youthful zeal, Teresa was also a typical child in many ways. She enjoyed playing games and socializing, particularly with her siblings, to whom she was very close. She had a strong, lively personality, and while her devotion to God was evident, she was also known for her love of books, stories, and spending time with friends. However, after her mother's death in 1529, when Teresa was just 14 years old, her spiritual journey took a more serious turn.

Beatriz's passing was a deeply emotional event for Teresa, and it left her feeling vulnerable and uncertain. In her grief, she turned to the Virgin Mary, asking her to be her mother in the absence of her earthly one. This moment marked a turning point in Teresa's life, solidifying her desire to dedicate herself more fully to God. She began to pray with more intensity and gradually withdrew from the worldly distractions of her youth.

Education and Intellectual Growth

After her mother's death, Teresa's father sent her to the Augustinian convent school of Santa María de Gracia in Ávila. It

7

was here that she received her formal education. The convent school was known for its strict adherence to discipline and religious instruction, and the environment helped nurture Teresa's growing desire to live a life devoted to God.

At the convent, Teresa encountered many influential texts, including works by early Christian mystics, which would later shape her own spiritual writings. She also developed a strong devotion to prayer and contemplation, though she struggled with her own weaknesses and temptations, often feeling torn between her love of the world and her desire for holiness. Her time at the convent left a lasting impact on her spiritual formation, introducing her to a life of religious discipline and prayer, though she would later describe this period as one of interior conflict.

Upon leaving the convent due to illness, Teresa returned home to recover, and it was during this period that she first seriously considered joining a religious order. She wrestled with the decision, as her natural inclination toward socializing and friendships made the prospect of the cloistered life difficult to embrace. Additionally, her father initially opposed the idea of her becoming a nun, preferring that she marry instead. Teresa, however, felt an increasingly strong pull toward the religious life, and after much internal struggle, she eventually decided to join the Carmelite Order.

Struggles with Worldly Influences

Teresa's entrance into the Carmelite convent of the Incarnation in 1535 was not without challenges. In her early years as a nun, she struggled to balance her spiritual aspirations with the more relaxed lifestyle of the convent. At the time, many Carmelite convents, including the one in Ávila, had adopted a more lenient approach to religious life, allowing nuns to receive visitors and engage in social activities. This relaxed atmosphere did not provide the spiritual rigor that Teresa sought, and for many years, she felt spiritually stagnant.

During this time, Teresa experienced a period of spiritual dryness, which she later described as a time when she felt distant from God. She was plagued by feelings of unworthiness and struggled to find the deep sense of devotion that had characterized her earlier years. These internal battles with temptation and distraction became a central theme in her later writings, where she emphasized the importance of perseverance in prayer, even during times of spiritual desolation.

Despite these early struggles, Teresa's devotion to God remained unwavering. Over time, she began to experience profound moments of spiritual awakening, which would later culminate in the mystical experiences that defined her later life. These early years of struggle and uncertainty, though difficult, were crucial in shaping the saint she would become, giving her the humility and self-awareness that would later become hallmarks of her teachings.

3

Entering the Carmelite Order

St. Teresa of Avila's decision to enter the Carmelite Order marked a significant turning point in her life, both spiritually and personally. After years of inner conflict, she ultimately chose to dedicate herself to the religious life, setting the stage for her later reforms and spiritual teachings. This chapter explores Teresa's entry into the convent, her early struggles with religious life, and the gradual deepening of her spiritual understanding that would eventually lead to her becoming a central figure in the Carmelite reform movement.

The Decision to Join the Carmelite Convent

By the time Teresa was in her early twenties, she was grappling with the tension between her worldly desires and her growing religious conviction. After leaving the Augustinian convent school of Santa María de Gracia due to illness, she returned home and spent several years contemplating her future. During this time, she wrestled with the expectations placed upon her by society and her family, particularly her father, who preferred that she marry rather than pursue a religious vocation.

However, Teresa's internal call to serve God became increasingly difficult to ignore. Her profound sense of guilt over her distractions and the allure of worldly pleasures weighed heavily on her. Despite her father's initial opposition, Teresa's resolve to embrace the religious life grew stronger. She later wrote about how deeply she desired to belong entirely to God, but also about how challenging it was to fully let go of her attachment to the world. This internal struggle would be a recurring theme throughout her spiritual journey.

In 1535, at the age of 20, Teresa made the decision to join the Carmelite convent of the Incarnation in Ávila. This convent, which housed about 150 nuns at the time, offered her

11

the opportunity to live a life dedicated to prayer, but it also allowed for some leniency in daily activities. The Carmelite Order was less strict than other orders, and while the convent provided spiritual refuge, it also permitted visitors and social engagements, something Teresa found appealing yet spiritually dangerous.

Early Years in the Carmelite Convent

Upon entering the Carmelite convent, Teresa's initial feelings were mixed. She had anticipated a life of deep religious devotion and prayer, but the reality of convent life in the 16th century was far less rigorous than she had expected. The nuns at the Incarnation were allowed to entertain visitors, attend social gatherings, and even receive gifts from outside the convent. Teresa found herself caught between her desire for a contemplative life and the distractions that these social engagements provided. This balance of spiritual discipline and lenient convent rules created an environment where Teresa felt she was drifting further from God, rather than drawing closer.

During her early years in the convent, Teresa faced a number of physical and spiritual trials. She suffered from frequent illnesses, one of which left her bedridden for almost three years. At one point, her condition became so severe that she fell into a coma, and her family even believed she had died. Miraculously, she recovered, but the experience left her with chronic health issues that would affect her for the rest of her life.

Physically weakened, Teresa also struggled spiritually during these years. She experienced what she later described as a "spiritual lukewarmness," where her prayer life was marked by distractions and lack of devotion. She felt torn between her duties as a nun and her continued attachment to worldly concerns. This spiritual dryness led to a period of deep frustration, as

Teresa could not seem to recapture the intense religious fervor of her youth. She later reflected that these early years in the convent were some of the most difficult of her life, filled with a sense of spiritual inertia and confusion.

The Influence of Spiritual Mentors and Books

Despite her struggles, Teresa continued to seek guidance on how to deepen her relationship with God. One of the most important influences during this time was her growing interest in the writings of Christian mystics. She began reading works by St. Augustine, St. Jerome, and other Church Fathers, whose writings on prayer and spiritual growth resonated with her own experiences. These texts provided Teresa with insights into the contemplative life and encouraged her to persevere in her spiritual quest.

In addition to her readings, Teresa sought out the advice of various spiritual directors and confessors, hoping to gain clarity in her relationship with God. However, she was often frustrated by the advice she received, as many of her confessors failed to understand the depth of her spiritual struggles. It was not until she met a Jesuit priest named Father Francisco de Borja that she began to receive the kind of spiritual guidance that helped her progress. Borja's counsel encouraged Teresa to focus on deepening her prayer life, even during times of spiritual dryness, and to seek God's presence within her own soul, rather than through external signs.

Spiritual Awakening and Mystical Experiences

In the midst of her spiritual struggles, Teresa began to experience profound mystical experiences, which would later define her spiritual legacy. These moments of deep spiritual insight came in the form of visions, inner locutions, and periods of intense prayer where she felt an overwhelming sense of God's presence. At first, Teresa was both elated and frightened by these experiences, unsure of their significance. Her fear was compounded by the skepticism of some of her confessors, who questioned the authenticity of her visions and warned her of potential spiritual deception.

However, Teresa soon came to understand that these mystical experiences were a gift from God, intended to draw her closer to Him. These moments of deep union with God became more frequent, and Teresa began to feel a renewed sense of purpose in her religious life. Her prayer life became more intense and focused, and she increasingly withdrew from the social distractions of convent life, dedicating more time to contemplation and spiritual reflection.

One of her most famous mystical experiences occurred when she saw a vision of an angel who pierced her heart with a flaming spear, symbolizing the intensity of her love for God. This experience, which she described in her autobiography *The Life of Teresa of Jesus*, left her with an overwhelming sense of divine love and solidified her commitment to a life of prayer and reform.

The Beginning of Reform

As Teresa's spiritual life deepened, so did her dissatisfaction with the state of the Carmelite convents. The lenient practices she had once tolerated now seemed to her a barrier to true contemplative prayer. She became convinced that the Carmelite Order needed to return to its original values of poverty, simplicity, and strict devotion to God. Her desire for reform would eventually lead her to found the Discalced Carmelite Order, which embraced a more austere way of life.

Teresa's early years in the convent were marked by inner conflict, spiritual dryness, and moments of profound mystical insight. These experiences shaped her understanding of prayer and spiritual growth, and they laid the foundation for the major reforms she would later undertake within the Carmelite Order. Her early struggles with worldly distractions and her eventual spiritual awakening became central themes in her later writings, offering guidance to others who sought to deepen their own relationship with God.

Teresa's entry into the Carmelite convent was not an immediate embrace of the rigorous spiritual life she would later advocate. Her early years were filled with physical ailments, spiritual struggles, and periods of doubt. Yet, it was through these challenges that Teresa began to develop her understanding of the importance of perseverance in prayer and the necessity of reforming the religious life. Her mystical experiences, though initially unsettling, became the key to unlocking her deeper relationship with God and would eventually inspire her to reform the Carmelite Order. These formative years in the convent were essential in shaping the future saint's journey toward spiritual leadership and reform.

4

The Mystical Visions

St. Teresa of Avila's mystical visions are among the most remarkable aspects of her life and spiritual legacy. These experiences of deep spiritual union with God were both transformative for Teresa herself and foundational to her role as a spiritual teacher and reformer. Teresa's mystical encounters were not just fleeting moments of divine insight; they were profound experiences that shaped her theology, her understanding of the soul's relationship with God, and her eventual reform of the Carmelite Order.

Early Mystical Experiences

Teresa's first mystical experiences occurred in her thirties, after a long period of spiritual dryness and internal conflict. For years, she struggled with distractions during prayer and felt distant from God. However, around the age of 39, Teresa began to experience what she called "consolations" or moments of profound peace and closeness to God during prayer. These were early signs of the mystical path she was about to embark on.

At first, Teresa was unsure of the authenticity of these experiences. In her autobiography, *The Life of Teresa of Jesus*, she describes feeling unworthy of such divine encounters and even feared that they were illusions or deceptions from the devil. She sought counsel from several confessors and spiritual directors, many of whom were skeptical of her experiences. Despite their doubts, Teresa felt an overwhelming sense of God's presence, which led her to continue deepening her prayer life.

The Rapture and Ecstasy

One of the most notable mystical phenomena Teresa experienced was the state of rapture or ecstasy. In this state, Teresa felt as though her soul was being drawn out of her body and toward God. She described it as a complete detachment from the

17

physical world, where her soul was consumed by the love and presence of God. These ecstasies often occurred unexpectedly during prayer or even in public, causing Teresa to levitate and lose consciousness for short periods.

Teresa's levitations, in particular, became well-known in her lifetime. Although they were awe-inspiring to witnesses, Teresa herself was often embarrassed by them. She prayed that God would not allow her to levitate in public, as she feared that others would think she was seeking attention or that her experiences were not genuine. Despite this, Teresa's levitations were viewed by many as signs of divine favor, further validating her mystical experiences.

In her writings, Teresa emphasized that these states of ecstasy were not something she sought or desired but were rather gifts from God. She warned others not to seek mystical experiences for their own sake, as true union with God is achieved through humility, perseverance in prayer, and self-surrender. For Teresa, mystical ecstasy was a direct result of God's grace, not human effort.

The Vision of the Angel and the Transverberation

One of Teresa's most famous mystical experiences is the *transverberation of the heart*, which occurred in the mid-1550s. In this vision, Teresa saw an angel holding a golden spear with a flaming tip. The angel pierced her heart with the spear, and she felt an overwhelming sense of divine love. Teresa described the experience as both intensely painful and ecstatic. The wound, she said, was not physical, but spiritual, leaving her with a deep and abiding love for God.

This vision of the angel is one of the most significant moments in Teresa's mystical life. The transverberation symbolized Teresa's total surrender to God's will and her complete union with Him. In her autobiography, she wrote that after the angel pierced her heart, she was left with a burning desire for God's love and an intense longing for heaven.

Artists and theologians have been captivated by Teresa's vision of the angel, and it has been depicted in numerous works of art, most famously in Gian Lorenzo Bernini's sculpture *The Ecstasy of Saint Teresa*, located in the Church of Santa Maria della Vittoria in Rome. This moment of divine encounter remains one of the defining symbols of Teresa's mystical journey and her profound love for God.

The Interior Castle and Spiritual Progression

Teresa's mystical experiences not only impacted her personally but also became the foundation for her spiritual teachings. In her most famous work, *The Interior Castle*, Teresa uses the metaphor of a castle with many rooms to describe the soul's journey toward union with God. This book, written in 1577, is a culmination of Teresa's own mystical experiences and offers a roadmap for others seeking spiritual perfection.

In *The Interior Castle*, Teresa describes the soul's progression through seven stages, or "mansions," each representing a deeper level of intimacy with God. The first mansions are marked by the soul's struggle with distractions and sin, while the later mansions represent stages of deeper contemplation and union with God. Teresa's mystical visions, particularly her experiences of ecstasy and the transverberation, correspond to the higher stages of the spiritual journey.

For Teresa, mystical experiences were not the end goal but rather milestones on the path to divine union. She emphasized that the journey toward God requires humility, self-knowledge, and detachment from worldly concerns. In the higher mansions, the soul becomes fully aligned with God's will and experiences a profound sense of peace and joy.

Visions of Christ and the Holy Trinity

In addition to her experience with the angel, Teresa also had numerous visions of Christ and the Holy Trinity. These visions were central to her spiritual life and gave her the strength to continue her reform efforts, even in the face of opposition. One of the most significant visions occurred in 1560 when Teresa saw Christ standing beside her. In this vision, Christ spoke to her, reassuring her of His presence and encouraging her to continue her work of reforming the Carmelite Order.

Teresa's visions of Christ were always accompanied by a deep sense of peace and certainty. She described these visions as moments when she felt closer to Christ than ever before, as if she could see Him with the eyes of her soul. These encounters with Christ became a source of comfort and guidance for Teresa, particularly during difficult times.

In one of her most profound mystical experiences, Teresa was granted a vision of the Holy Trinity. This vision, which she described as beyond words, gave her a deeper understanding of the mystery of God's nature. For Teresa, the vision of the Trinity was the ultimate expression of divine love and unity, and it left her with a lasting sense of awe and reverence for God's majesty.

Teresa's Struggles with Skepticism and Criticism

Throughout her life, Teresa faced significant skepticism and criticism regarding her mystical experiences. Many of her contemporaries, including some of her confessors, doubted the authenticity of her visions. In 16th-century Spain, mystical experiences were often viewed with suspicion, particularly for women. The Inquisition was active during Teresa's lifetime, and the Church closely monitored anyone who claimed to have visions or direct experiences with God.

Despite these challenges, Teresa remained steadfast in her belief that her visions were genuine encounters with God. She documented her experiences in her writings, not to glorify herself, but to offer guidance to others on the path to divine union. Her humility and perseverance in the face of doubt are evident in her works, where she often downplayed her own role in the mystical encounters and emphasized God's grace as the true source of her experiences.

Teresa's spiritual advisors, including St. John of the Cross, eventually validated her experiences, and her writings were approved by the Church. Nevertheless, she continued to face opposition throughout her life, particularly from those who were resistant to her reforms of the Carmelite Order. Despite the obstacles, Teresa's unwavering faith and commitment to her mystical path allowed her to overcome these challenges and leave a lasting impact on Christian spirituality.

The Significance of Teresa's Mystical Visions

Teresa's mystical visions were not isolated events but were deeply integrated into her spiritual life and theological teachings. These experiences provided her with a profound understanding of the nature of God and the soul's journey toward divine union. Her visions of Christ, the Holy Trinity, and the angel were not merely personal experiences but were expressions of her deepening relationship with God.

For Teresa, the ultimate goal of the mystical life was union with God. Her mystical experiences, particularly her ecstasies and the transverberation of the heart, were manifestations of this union. These experiences taught her that true spiritual growth requires complete surrender to God's will, detachment from worldly desires, and perseverance in prayer.

Teresa's mystical insights also had a profound impact on the reform of the Carmelite Order. Her deep sense of God's presence inspired her to create a more austere and contemplative way of life for her fellow nuns. The Discalced Carmelite Order, which Teresa founded, embraced a strict rule of poverty, silence, and prayer, allowing its members to focus entirely on their relationship with God.

5

Reforms of the Carmelite Order

St. Teresa of Avila's reform of the Carmelite Order is one of her most enduring legacies. Deeply dissatisfied with the laxity and lack of spiritual discipline she observed in her own convent and others across Spain, Teresa felt a divine calling to return the Carmelite Order to its original principles of austerity, contemplation, and simplicity. Her efforts were met with resistance and opposition, both from within the Carmelite community and from external forces, yet her determination, perseverance, and faith led to the establishment of the Discalced Carmelite Order. This chapter details the process of reform, the challenges she faced, and the lasting impact of her work on the Church.

The State of the Carmelite Order in the 16th Century

During Teresa's time, the Carmelite Order, like many religious orders in Europe, had grown increasingly lenient in its practices. Founded in the 12th century by hermits living on Mount Carmel in the Holy Land, the Carmelites had originally embraced a life of prayer, solitude, and poverty. However, by the 16th century, many Carmelite convents and monasteries in Spain had adopted more relaxed rules. Nuns were allowed to entertain visitors, own personal property, and receive gifts. The original spirit of simplicity and contemplative prayer had, in many places, given way to a more social and comfortable lifestyle.

In the convent of the Incarnation in Ávila, where Teresa lived, there were about 150 nuns, far more than the convent was designed to support. The large number of nuns, combined with the relaxed rules, created an environment where true contemplative prayer and devotion to God were difficult to maintain. Teresa herself struggled with distractions and found it challenging to focus on her spiritual growth amid the social activities and obligations of convent life.

For years, Teresa endured this environment, feeling torn between her desire for a deeper relationship with God and the worldly distractions around her. However, after experiencing profound mystical encounters, Teresa became convinced that the Carmelite Order needed to return to its roots. She believed that only through a stricter observance of the Carmelite Rule could nuns and monks fully dedicate themselves to God and experience true union with Him.

The Birth of the Discalced Carmelites

The turning point came in 1562, when Teresa received approval from Pope Pius IV to found a new convent that would adhere to a more rigorous interpretation of the Carmelite Rule. This new convent, named St. Joseph's, was established in Ávila with only a handful of nuns who shared Teresa's vision of a life devoted to prayer, poverty, and simplicity. The word "Discalced" means "barefoot," symbolizing the nuns' commitment to humility and poverty, as they wore simple sandals rather than shoes.

The founding of St. Joseph's was not without controversy. Many within the Carmelite Order, as well as influential figures in Ávila, opposed Teresa's reforms. Some believed that her insistence on stricter rules was unnecessary, while others accused her of disobedience and ambition. The establishment of a new, reformed convent was seen by some as a challenge to the existing Carmelite institutions, and Teresa faced considerable resistance from both religious and secular authorities.

Despite the opposition, Teresa remained resolute in her mission. She believed that God had called her to restore the Carmelite Order to its original purity, and she trusted that He would provide the support she needed. Over time, Teresa gained the backing of key figures in the Church, including Father Jerónimo Gracián and St. John of the Cross, a fellow mystic and reformer. With their help, Teresa began to expand her reform efforts beyond Ávila.

Expansion of the Reform Movement

After the successful establishment of St. Joseph's, Teresa's reform movement began to gain momentum. Between 1567 and 1582, she traveled throughout Spain, founding new Discalced Carmelite convents and monasteries. In total, she established 17 new convents and several monasteries for Discalced Carmelite monks, who shared the same commitment to a life of poverty, prayer, and solitude.

Teresa's reforms extended not only to the lifestyle of the nuns and monks but also to the governance of the convents and monasteries. She believed in small, tightly-knit communities where the nuns and monks could support each other in their spiritual journey. Each convent was to be self-sustaining and free from the influence of wealthy patrons, who had often interfered in the affairs of religious houses. Teresa also emphasized the importance of humility and mutual respect within the community, insisting that all members, regardless of their status or background, be treated equally.

One of Teresa's most significant collaborations was with St. John of the Cross, who shared her vision for a reformed Carmelite Order. In 1568, St. John founded the first Discalced Carmelite monastery for men in Duruelo. Like Teresa, St. John believed in the importance of returning to the original spirit of the Carmelite Rule, and together they worked to establish a network of reformed convents and monasteries throughout Spain.

Opposition and Challenges

Teresa's efforts to reform the Carmelite Order were met with considerable resistance, both from within the Carmelite community and from external authorities. Many of the traditional Carmelite convents and monasteries viewed Teresa's reforms as a threat to their way of life. Some accused her of pride and disobedience, arguing that her insistence on stricter rules was unnecessary and divisive.

The opposition was not limited to members of the Carmelite Order. Secular authorities, including city officials and local aristocrats, also opposed Teresa's reforms. In many cases, these individuals had financial or social ties to the existing convents and monasteries, and they viewed Teresa's efforts to establish independent, self-sustaining communities as a threat to their influence.

One of the most significant challenges Teresa faced came from the Carmelite hierarchy itself. In 1575, the General Chapter of the Carmelite Order, held in Piacenza, Italy, issued a decree that sought to suppress the Discalced Carmelites and place them under the authority of the traditional Carmelite superiors. This decree threatened to undo all of Teresa's work and return the reformed convents and monasteries to the more relaxed practices of the unreformed Carmelites.

Undeterred, Teresa appealed to King Philip II of Spain, who was sympathetic to her cause. With his support, she took her case to Pope Gregory XIII, who ultimately issued a papal bull in 1580 granting the Discalced Carmelites autonomy from the traditional Carmelite Order. This victory allowed Teresa to continue her reform efforts without interference from the unreformed Carmelites and solidified the future of the Discalced Carmelite Order.

Teresa's Vision for the Carmelite Life

At the heart of Teresa's reform movement was her vision for a life of prayer, poverty, and contemplation. She believed that the purpose of the Carmelite vocation was to seek union with God through a life of interior prayer and solitude. The distractions of wealth, social obligations, and worldly concerns, she argued, prevented nuns and monks from fully dedicating themselves to this purpose.

In her writings, particularly *The Way of Perfection*, Teresa laid out her vision for the reformed Carmelite life. She emphasized the importance of humility, self-denial, and reliance on God's grace. Teresa also taught that prayer was not just a duty but a way of life. She encouraged her nuns to practice both mental prayer (interior, contemplative prayer) and vocal prayer (the recitation of traditional prayers), always striving for a deeper relationship with God.

Teresa's reforms also placed a strong emphasis on community life. She believed that the convent should be a place of mutual support, where the nuns could help each other grow in holiness. This communal aspect of Carmelite life was essential to Teresa's vision, as she saw the convent as both a spiritual sanctuary and a place of refuge from the distractions of the outside world.

Legacy of the Discalced Carmelites

Teresa of Avila's reforms had a lasting impact on the Carmelite Order and on Christian spirituality more broadly. The Discalced Carmelites, both the nuns and the friars, became known for their commitment to a life of prayer, poverty, and contemplation. Teresa's teachings on prayer and the spiritual life, particularly as expressed in *The Interior Castle* and *The Way of Perfection*, have become foundational texts for Christian mysticism and continue to inspire believers today.

The Discalced Carmelites quickly spread beyond Spain, with

new convents and monasteries being established across Europe and eventually around the world. The order became known for its deep commitment to contemplative prayer and its emphasis on spiritual discipline. Teresa's reforms helped revitalize the Carmelite Order at a time when many religious orders were struggling with laxity and secular influences.

In 1970, St. Teresa of Avila was declared a Doctor of the Church by Pope Paul VI, recognizing her profound contributions to Christian theology and spirituality. Her reforms not only restored the Carmelite Order to its original purpose but also left a legacy of spiritual depth and discipline that continues to influence the Church today.

Conclusion

St. Teresa of Avila's reform of the Carmelite Order was a monumental achievement, rooted in her deep desire to return religious life to its original principles of poverty, prayer, and simplicity. Despite facing significant opposition from both within the Church and from secular authorities, Teresa's un-wavering faith and commitment to her mission allowed her to succeed in founding the Discalced Carmelite Order. Her vision for a life of contemplative prayer, communal support, and reliance on God's grace has left an indelible mark on Christian spirituality. Through her reforms, Teresa not only revitalized the Carmelite Order but also provided a model of spiritual dedication that continues to inspire believers to this day.

6

Major Spiritual Works

St. Teresa of Avila is renowned not only for her mystical experiences and reforms within the Carmelite Order but also for her prolific spiritual writings. Her works have become foundational texts in Christian mysticism and have earned her the title of Doctor of the Church. Teresa's three major works—The Life of Teresa of Jesus, The Way of Perfection, and The Interior Castle—each offer profound insights into the spiritual journey, providing practical guidance for those seeking a deeper relationship with God. These writings reflect her experiences, her understanding of the soul's path to God, and her theological vision, all of which have shaped Christian spirituality for centuries.

The Life of Teresa of Jesus

Written in 1562, *The Life of Teresa of Jesus* (also known as her autobiography) is one of the earliest and most intimate accounts of St. Teresa's spiritual development. It was written at the request of her confessor, Father García de Toledo, and offers a firsthand look at her life, her mystical experiences, and her thoughts on the challenges of living a life devoted to God. The autobiography is a blend of personal reflection, theological insight, and practical spiritual advice, making it both an inspiring and instructive text.

The book is divided into several sections, each focusing on different aspects of Teresa's life, from her childhood to her entry into the Carmelite convent, her mystical visions, and her efforts to reform the order. In the early chapters, Teresa describes her struggles with spiritual distractions and the tensions between her desire for a worldly life and her calling to serve God. This tension is a recurring theme in the book, and Teresa's reflections on it provide valuable lessons for anyone who struggles with balancing their spiritual and worldly lives.

One of the most significant sections of *The Life* is Teresa's detailed account of her mystical experiences, including her famous vision of the angel piercing her heart with a flaming spear (the transverberation). These experiences were deeply personal and transformative for Teresa, and they became the foundation for her spiritual teachings. In the later chapters, Teresa shifts from autobiographical reflection to offering practical advice on prayer and the spiritual life, emphasizing the importance of humility, perseverance, and reliance on God's grace.

Throughout *The Life*, Teresa's humility and self-awareness shine through. She often downplays her own spiritual achievements, attributing them entirely to God's grace. Her candid descriptions of her struggles, doubts, and failures make her an accessible and relatable spiritual guide. *The Life of Teresa of Jesus* not only provides insight into the mind of one of the greatest Christian mystics but also offers timeless advice for anyone seeking to deepen their relationship with God.

The Way of Perfection

The Way of Perfection, written between 1565 and 1566, is another of Teresa's most important spiritual works. This book was written specifically for the nuns of the reformed Carmelite convents, particularly those at the newly founded convent of St. Joseph's in Ávila. Its purpose was to guide them in living a life of prayer, humility, and spiritual perfection. However, *The Way of Perfection* is not only relevant to nuns but to all Christians seeking a deeper understanding of the spiritual life.

The book is divided into 42 chapters, and it begins with Teresa's reflections on the challenges facing the Carmelite Order and the world in general. She wrote *The Way of Perfection* at a time when the Church was under threat from the Protestant

Reformation, and she saw her efforts to reform the Carmelite Order as part of a broader spiritual renewal within the Church. In the opening chapters, Teresa emphasizes the importance of prayer, both vocal and mental, as the foundation for a life of spiritual growth. She also addresses the practical challenges of community life, urging her nuns to practice humility, obedience, and charity toward one another.

One of the central themes of *The Way of Perfection* is Teresa's teaching on prayer. She provides detailed instructions on how to practice mental prayer, which involves deep contemplation and focusing the mind on God's presence. Teresa explains that prayer is not about saying many words but about cultivating a deep relationship with God through love and humility. She warns her readers not to be discouraged by distractions or dryness in prayer, as these are common experiences on the spiritual journey. Instead, she encourages perseverance and trust in God's grace.

Another key theme in *The Way of Perfection* is the importance of detachment from worldly concerns. Teresa teaches that spiritual perfection requires a complete surrender of one's will to God and a detachment from material possessions, personal desires, and even one's own reputation. She emphasizes that humility is the foundation of all virtue and that true humility involves recognizing one's dependence on God for everything.

Throughout the book, Teresa's tone is both practical and encouraging. She speaks as a mother to her spiritual daughters, offering them wisdom, guidance, and reassurance. *The Way of Perfection* remains a valuable resource for anyone seeking to grow in prayer and deepen their relationship with God.

The Interior Castle

The Interior Castle, written in 1577, is widely regarded as St.

Teresa's masterpiece and one of the greatest works of Christian mysticism. In this book, Teresa presents a comprehensive guide to the spiritual journey, using the metaphor of a castle to describe the soul's progression toward union with God. The castle has seven mansions, each representing a different stage of spiritual growth, with the innermost mansion symbolizing the deepest union with God.

In *The Interior Castle*, Teresa describes the soul as a beautiful and radiant castle made of crystal, in which there are many rooms, or mansions. The soul's journey begins in the outermost mansions, where it is still heavily influenced by the world and by sin. As the soul progresses inward, it becomes more purified and more focused on God, eventually reaching the seventh mansion, where it experiences perfect union with Him.

The first three mansions represent the stages of the active spiritual life, where the soul is still struggling with sin and distractions. In these mansions, Teresa emphasizes the importance of self-knowledge, humility, and the practice of virtue. She teaches that spiritual progress requires a deep awareness of one's own weaknesses and a reliance on God's grace to overcome them.

The fourth, fifth, and sixth mansions represent the stages of the contemplative life, where the soul begins to experience deeper prayer and greater intimacy with God. In these mansions, the soul undergoes profound transformations, often experiencing mystical phenomena such as raptures, ecstasies, and visions. However, Teresa warns that these experiences are not the goal of the spiritual life and should not be sought for their own sake. Instead, they are gifts from God that help the soul grow in love and humility.

The seventh mansion, the final stage of the spiritual journey, represents the soul's perfect union with God. In this mansion, the soul experiences a profound sense of peace and joy, as it is completely united with God's will. Teresa describes this union as a spiritual marriage, where the soul and God become one in love. This stage of the spiritual journey is marked by a deep sense of inner freedom and a total surrender to God's will.

The Interior Castle is not just a theoretical treatise on mysticism; it is a practical guide for anyone seeking to grow in their relationship with God. Teresa's detailed descriptions of the different stages of the spiritual journey, along with her practical advice on prayer and self-discipline, make this book an invaluable resource for spiritual seekers. Her central message is that the journey toward union with God requires perseverance, humility, and a deep trust in God's grace.

Core Themes and Teachings in Her Writings

Across all of her major works, several core themes emerge that define St. Teresa's spiritual teachings:

1. **Humility and Self-Knowledge**: Teresa consistently emphasizes the importance of humility as the foundation of the spiritual life. She teaches that true humility involves recognizing one's dependence on God and being honest about one's weaknesses and sins. Self-knowledge is crucial for spiritual growth, as it allows individuals to understand their faults and rely more fully on God's grace.

2. **The Centrality of Prayer**: Prayer is at the heart of Teresa's spiritual teachings. She advocates both vocal prayer (traditional prayers) and mental prayer (silent, contemplative prayer), with a particular emphasis on the latter. Teresa's concept of prayer is deeply relational—prayer is not about saying many words but about cultivating a deep, loving

relationship with God. Her writings provide practical advice on how to overcome distractions, dryness, and other obstacles in prayer.

3. **The Journey Toward Union with God**: In all her major works, Teresa presents the spiritual life as a journey toward union with God. Whether through the metaphor of the interior castle or the stages of prayer, Teresa teaches that the soul's ultimate goal is to be united with God's will. This journey requires perseverance, detachment from worldly concerns, and a complete surrender to God.

4. **The Role of Suffering and Purification**: Teresa's writings reflect her belief that suffering and trials are an essential part of the spiritual journey. She teaches that the soul must be purified through suffering in order to grow in virtue and become more closely united with God. However, she also emphasizes that God's grace is always present to help individuals endure these trials and find joy in their suffering.

5. **Love as the Basis of All Virtue**: For Teresa, love is the driving force behind all spiritual progress. Love for God and love for others is the foundation of the Christian life, and all virtues are rooted in this love. Teresa teaches that the deeper one's love for God, the more easily one can overcome sin and grow in holiness.

7

Teresa's Teachings on Prayer

St. Teresa of Avila is widely regarded as one of the foremost teachers of Christian prayer. Her profound experiences in prayer and her practical advice have made her writings foundational in the development of Christian spirituality. In her major works, including The Life of Teresa of Jesus, The Way of Perfection, and The Interior Castle, Teresa offers clear and insightful guidance on the practice of prayer, emphasizing the transformative power of cultivating a deep relationship with God through prayer. This chapter explores Teresa's teachings on prayer, focusing on the four stages of prayer, the distinction between meditation and contemplation, and her insights on achieving union with God.

The Four Stages of Prayer

St. Teresa of Avila outlines four stages of prayer in her writings, providing a structured pathway for spiritual progress. These stages represent the soul's progression from simple vocal prayer to the profound experience of union with God. Teresa's stages are not rigid steps that one must follow in a linear fashion, but rather a description of the natural development of one's prayer life as one grows in intimacy with God.

1. **The First Stage: Mental Prayer or Meditation** The first stage of prayer is what Teresa refers to as "mental prayer," which she often equates with meditation. In this stage, the soul actively engages the mind and heart in reflecting on God, His works, and His Word. Meditation involves concentrating on a specific theme, such as Christ's Passion, the life of the saints, or passages from Scripture. It is a process of thinking deeply about divine truths and their implications for the soul.

2. Teresa emphasizes that this stage requires effort and discipline. Distractions are common, and it can be difficult to maintain focus. However, Teresa encourages perseverance, teaching that even the simplest acts of focusing the mind on God can be deeply pleasing to Him. Mental prayer is also the foundation for developing a deeper relationship with God, as it trains the soul to move beyond mere recitation of words to a more intimate engagement with the divine.

3. In this stage, the individual must actively work to keep the mind centered on God. The soul's love and desire for God are awakened and strengthened, and through meditation, one begins to form a closer bond with God, though the experience may still feel distant or intellectual.

4. **The Second Stage: The Prayer of Quiet** As the soul progresses in prayer, it may experience what Teresa calls the "prayer of quiet." This is the second stage, in which God begins to take a more active role in the prayer. While the individual still engages in mental prayer, the soul begins to experience moments of deep peace and tranquility, which Teresa describes as a "gentle drawing inward." In this state, the will becomes captivated by God, even though the mind may still be distracted or active.

5. The prayer of quiet is characterized by an increased sense of God's presence, and the soul feels a deepening sense of love and awe for Him. Teresa explains that while distractions may still arise, the soul no longer needs to exert the same level of effort to focus on God. Instead, God draws the soul into a state of peace and quietness. This stage represents a more passive form of prayer, where the soul is receiving more from God than it is giving.

6. Teresa emphasizes that the prayer of quiet is a gift from

God, not something that can be achieved through human effort alone. She advises humility and trust in God's timing, as the experience of quiet prayer cannot be forced or controlled. The soul should accept these moments of divine intimacy with gratitude and not be concerned if they come and go.

7. **The Third Stage: The Prayer of Union** In the third stage, known as the "prayer of union," the soul experiences a deeper and more intense connection with God. In this stage, Teresa teaches that the faculties of the soul—especially the intellect and memory—become completely absorbed in God. The soul's awareness of the world and its distractions diminishes, and it experiences a profound sense of closeness with God. Teresa describes this state as one where the soul feels "engulfed" by God's love, as though the individual's will and God's will are fully united.

8. In the prayer of union, the soul is almost completely passive, as it experiences a direct infusion of grace and love from God. Teresa explains that this state is beyond words and beyond the soul's ability to fully comprehend. The experience of union brings a deep sense of joy, peace, and love, as the soul feels it is fully resting in God's presence.

9. Teresa warns, however, that the prayer of union may be brief and is often accompanied by trials and spiritual dryness once it has passed. These moments of darkness are allowed by God to further purify the soul and deepen its dependence on Him. While the prayer of union is a deeply consoling experience, Teresa cautions against becoming attached to it. True spiritual progress comes not from seeking such consolations, but from a consistent life of virtue, humility, and prayer.

40

10. **The Fourth Stage: The Prayer of Ecstasy or Rapture** The final stage of prayer, according to Teresa, is the "prayer of ecstasy" or "rapture." In this stage, the soul is completely absorbed in God, to the point that it is unaware of anything happening around it. Teresa describes this experience as a complete detachment from the senses and from the physical world, where the soul is lifted into a state of pure contemplation of God.

11. During the prayer of ecstasy, the soul may experience physical effects, such as the sensation of levitation or an overwhelming sense of divine love. These experiences are often accompanied by feelings of intense joy and longing for God. Teresa explains that the soul in this state desires nothing but to be with God and is completely detached from earthly concerns.

12. The prayer of ecstasy is the closest the soul can come to experiencing union with God while still in this life. However, Teresa cautions that this stage is also accompanied by spiritual trials and periods of darkness. She teaches that God allows these trials to purify the soul and prepare it for an even deeper union with Him.

Meditation and Contemplation

St. Teresa of Avila distinguishes between two important forms of prayer: **meditation** and **contemplation**. Both are vital to the spiritual life, but they represent different stages of the soul's journey toward God.

- **Meditation**: Meditation, or mental prayer, is the first stage of prayer and involves the active use of the mind. In meditation, the individual reflects on divine truths, such as the life of Christ, the mysteries of the rosary, or passages from Scripture. The goal of meditation is to deepen one's understanding of God and to stir the heart toward love and devotion.

· Teresa explains that meditation requires effort and discipline, especially for beginners. It is often challenging to keep the mind focused, and distractions are common. However, she encourages perseverance, teaching that even imperfect efforts at meditation are valuable in the eyes of God. Through consistent practice, the soul gradually becomes more attuned to God's presence and more capable of entering deeper stages of prayer.

· **Contemplation**: As the soul progresses in prayer, it may begin to experience what Teresa calls "contemplation." Contemplation is a more passive form of prayer, in which the soul no longer actively engages the mind but simply rests in God's presence. In contemplation, the individual moves beyond thoughts and words, entering into a state of silent communion with God.

· Teresa explains that contemplation is a gift from God, not something that can be achieved through human effort. It often comes unexpectedly, and the soul should receive it with humility and gratitude. Contemplation represents a deepening of the soul's relationship with God, where the individual no longer needs to strive for connection but is drawn into God's presence by His grace.

· One of the key differences between meditation and contemplation is that meditation involves active mental engagement, while contemplation is marked by passivity and stillness. Teresa teaches that both forms of prayer are essential to the spiritual life and that the soul should be open to whichever form of prayer God grants at a given time.

Insights on Union with God

One of St. Teresa's most profound contributions to Christian spirituality is her teaching on the soul's union with God. Throughout her writings, she describes union with God as the ultimate goal of the spiritual life, a state in which the soul's will becomes completely aligned with God's will, and the individual experiences a profound sense of peace, love, and joy.

Teresa's teachings on union with God are deeply rooted in her own mystical experiences. She describes union as a "spiritual marriage" between the soul and God, where the two become one in love. This union is the culmination of the soul's journey through the stages of prayer, and it represents the highest form of intimacy with God that can be experienced in this life.

- **Spiritual Marriage**: In *The Interior Castle*, Teresa uses the metaphor of spiritual marriage to describe the soul's union with God. She explains that just as a married couple becomes one in love, so too does the soul become one with God in spiritual marriage. In this state, the soul experiences perfect peace and joy, as it is fully united with God's will.
- Teresa emphasizes that spiritual marriage is not something that can be achieved through human effort alone. It is a gift from God, granted to the soul that has been purified through prayer, suffering, and self-denial. The soul in this state no longer desires anything but God and is completely detached from the world.
- **The Role of Humility and Detachment**: Throughout her teachings on union with God, Teresa stresses the importance of humility and detachment. She teaches that the soul

43

cannot achieve union with God if it is still attached to worldly concerns or if it is seeking spiritual consolations for their own sake. True union with God requires a complete surrender of the will and a deep sense of humility, recognizing one's dependence on God for everything.

- Teresa's insights on union with God are not just for mystics or those who experience extraordinary spiritual phenomena. She teaches that all souls are called to union with God and that this union is attainable through a life of prayer, humility, and love. Her writings offer practical guidance for anyone seeking a deeper relationship with God, emphasizing that union with Him is the ultimate goal of the spiritual life.

8

Teresa's Role in the Counter-Reformation

St. Teresa of Avila's life and work coincided with one of the most turbulent periods in the history of the Catholic Church: the Counter-Reformation. This movement, which began in the mid-16th century, was the Church's response to the Protestant Reformation, which had sparked widespread religious, political, and social upheaval across Europe. The Catholic Church sought to address internal corruption, clarify its doctrines, and reaffirm its authority in the face of growing Protestant influence. In this context, Teresa of Avila emerged as one of the most significant spiritual leaders of the Catholic Counter-Reformation, playing a critical role in renewing and strengthening Catholic spirituality.

Her Influence on the Church

St. Teresa's influence on the Catholic Church during the Counter-Reformation was profound, not only through her personal reforms of the Carmelite Order but also through her writings and spiritual teachings, which became a cornerstone of Catholic mysticism and spirituality. Her works, particularly *The Interior Castle* and *The Way of Perfection*, were deeply theological and provided the Church with a framework for understanding prayer, contemplative life, and the soul's union with God, all of which were vital during a time when the Church was being challenged from within and without.

The Protestant Reformation, which began in 1517 with Martin Luther's 95 Theses, called into question many practices of the Catholic Church, including the veneration of saints, the efficacy of the sacraments, and the value of monastic life. Protestant reformers argued for a more direct and personal relationship with God, criticizing the perceived spiritual laxity and corruption of the clergy. In contrast, Teresa's reforms and

46

teachings within the Catholic tradition provided a clear and compelling example of how personal holiness, prayer, and a life of asceticism could lead to deep spiritual renewal within the existing structures of the Church.

One of the key ways Teresa influenced the Church was through her insistence on the importance of interior, contemplative prayer. At a time when the Catholic Church was focusing on defending its external practices and doctrines, Teresa reminded the faithful of the importance of an interior life centered on personal devotion and direct communication with God. Her teaching that prayer was essential for the soul's union with God helped revitalize the spiritual lives of many Catholics, particularly those within religious orders.

Additionally, Teresa's reform of the Carmelite Order, with its emphasis on poverty, humility, and a return to the original austere rule of the order, served as a model for other monastic reforms throughout Europe. The Discalced Carmelite Order that she founded, with the help of St. John of the Cross, became a symbol of spiritual renewal and commitment to the Catholic faith. Teresa's reformed Carmelite convents became centers of prayer, education, and missionary work, contributing to the Church's efforts to restore discipline and fervor among its clergy and laity.

Support from the Catholic Hierarchy

Despite the initial opposition Teresa faced from some members of the Carmelite Order and local authorities, her reform efforts eventually gained the support of influential figures within the Catholic hierarchy. Teresa's persistence, combined with her deep spiritual insights and evident sanctity, helped her win the backing of key Church leaders, including bishops, cardinals, and even the Spanish monarchy, which played a significant role in her eventual success.

King Philip II of Spain, one of the most powerful monarchs of the era and a staunch defender of the Catholic faith, became an important supporter of Teresa's reforms. Philip II recognized the importance of revitalizing monastic life and saw in Teresa's efforts a way to strengthen the Church's spiritual foundation during a time of great upheaval. His support helped protect Teresa and her newly founded Discalced Carmelite convents from attempts by the unreformed Carmelites to suppress her work.

Teresa also gained the favor of several prominent Church officials, including Father Jerónimo Gracián, who became one of her closest collaborators and spiritual directors. Father Gracián was instrumental in helping Teresa expand her reforms and establish new convents across Spain. His influence within the Church hierarchy, along with his deep respect for Teresa's spiritual wisdom, allowed her to navigate the complex politics of Church reform and gain the necessary permissions to continue her work.

One of the most significant milestones in Teresa's reform efforts came in 1580, when Pope Gregory XIII issued a papal bull granting the Discalced Carmelites official recognition as an independent branch of the Carmelite Order. This papal approval was a turning point for Teresa, as it solidified her reforms and ensured their continuation beyond her lifetime. With the support of the papacy, the Discalced Carmelites were able to expand their influence across Europe, becoming a vital force in the Church's spiritual renewal.

Teresa's success in gaining the support of the Catholic hierarchy was due in part to her ability to balance her deep mystical experiences with practical, down-to-earth leadership. While her visions and mystical experiences were extraordinary, Teresa always emphasized the importance of humility, obedience, and adherence to Church authority. This combination of personal holiness and institutional loyalty made her a trusted figure within the Church, even among those who were initially skeptical of her mystical experiences.

Teresa's Role in Strengthening Catholic Spirituality

Teresa's contributions to the Counter-Reformation went far beyond the structural reforms of the Carmelite Order. Her writings and teachings on prayer, spirituality, and the nature of the soul had a lasting impact on Catholic thought, helping to reinvigorate the Church's spiritual life at a time when it was under intense scrutiny.

1. **The Interior Life and Contemplative Prayer:** One of Teresa's most significant contributions to Catholic spirituality was her teaching on the interior life and contemplative prayer. At a time when the Church was defending its external rites and sacraments against Protestant criticism, Teresa emphasized that true spiritual renewal must begin within the soul. Her writings on the stages of prayer, particularly in *The Interior Castle*, offered Catholics a roadmap for deepening their relationship with God through personal, contemplative prayer.

2. Teresa's emphasis on the soul's direct experience of God through prayer aligned with the broader goals of the Counter-Reformation, which sought to reawaken the spiritual fervor of the faithful. By encouraging Catholics to cultivate an inner life of prayer and contemplation, Teresa helped create a foundation for the spiritual renewal that was so desperately needed in the wake of the Protestant

Reformation. Her teachings on prayer became a counter-balance to Protestant critiques of the Catholic Church's reliance on external rituals, showing that the Catholic tradition also valued personal, interior communion with God.

3. **Spiritual Discernment and Mysticism**: Another key aspect of Teresa's role in strengthening Catholic spirituality was her emphasis on spiritual discernment. In her writings, Teresa provided detailed guidance on how to discern the authenticity of mystical experiences and how to avoid spiritual deception. Her clear, practical advice on discerning the difference between true and false visions was essential in an era when both the Catholic Church and its Protestant critics were wary of mystical phenomena.

4. Teresa's focus on spiritual discernment reassured Church authorities that her mystical experiences were genuine and aligned with Catholic doctrine. By grounding her mystical teachings in orthodox theology, Teresa demonstrated that deep mystical experiences could coexist with a strong commitment to Church tradition. Her writings helped the Church navigate the complexities of mysticism during the Counter-Reformation, providing a framework for understanding and validating authentic mystical experiences while rejecting those that were not in line with Catholic teaching.

5. **Reforming Monastic Life**: Teresa's reform of the Carmelite Order was part of a broader effort to renew monastic life throughout the Catholic Church. During the Counter-Reformation, the Church recognized that many religious orders had become lax in their practices and that monastic life needed to be revitalized if it was

to serve as a model of holiness for the rest of the Church. Teresa's emphasis on poverty, simplicity, and prayer within the reformed Carmelite convents became a model for other religious orders seeking to return to their original charisms.

6. Teresa's reforms also had a missionary dimension. The Discalced Carmelites, both nuns and friars, became active participants in the Church's efforts to spread the Catholic faith in newly colonized regions and among the faithful in Europe. Their dedication to prayer and contemplation gave them the spiritual strength to serve as missionaries, educators, and spiritual guides during a time of great religious upheaval. In this way, Teresa's reforms not only revitalized monastic life but also contributed to the Church's broader efforts to evangelize and defend the faith during the Counter-Reformation.

7. **A Model of Female Leadership**: Teresa's role in the Counter-Reformation was also significant because of her status as a female leader in a male-dominated Church. At a time when women's roles in the Church were limited, Teresa emerged as a powerful spiritual authority whose influence extended far beyond her convent walls. Her ability to navigate the complex political and ecclesiastical structures of the Church while remaining deeply faithful to her vocation as a Carmelite nun made her a model of female leadership in the Church.

8. Teresa's writings on the spiritual life have continued to inspire both men and women in their pursuit of holiness. Her emphasis on humility, obedience, and trust in God's grace resonates with anyone seeking a deeper relationship with God, regardless of their gender or state in life. By

demonstrating that women could play a crucial role in the Church's spiritual renewal, Teresa helped pave the way for future generations of women to contribute to the life of the Church in significant ways.

St. Teresa of Avila's role in the Counter-Reformation was multifaceted and deeply influential. Through her reforms of the Carmelite Order, her spiritual writings, and her personal example of holiness, Teresa helped strengthen the Catholic Church during a time of great crisis. Her teachings on prayer, interior life, and spiritual discernment provided a roadmap for Catholics seeking to deepen their relationship with God, while her reform of monastic life became a model for the renewal of religious orders throughout Europe.

Teresa's impact on the Church went far beyond her own lifetime. Her writings continue to be studied and revered as some of the most important works of Christian mysticism, and her reforms within the Carmelite Order helped revitalize the Church's spiritual foundation during one of the most challenging periods in its history. Through her life and work, St. Teresa of Avila played a critical role in the Catholic Church's efforts to reaffirm its spiritual authority and guide the faithful through the turbulent waters of the Counter-Reformation.

40

9

Final Years and Legacy

St. Teresa of Avila's final years were marked by physical suffering, unrelenting dedication to the reform of the Carmelite Order, and a deepening of her mystical relationship with God. Despite the exhaustion and illness that plagued her toward the end of her life, Teresa continued to travel across Spain, establishing new Discalced Carmelite convents and monasteries. Her final years, though challenging, solidified her spiritual legacy, and her influence only grew after her death. Teresa's canonization, her recognition as a Doctor of the Church, and her continued impact on Christian spirituality ensure that her legacy remains alive and vibrant in both the Church and beyond.

Teresa's Death and Canonization

By 1582, St. Teresa's health had deteriorated significantly due to the immense physical and emotional toll of her reform efforts. For years, she had traveled extensively, founding convents and monasteries across Spain, despite suffering from a range of health issues, including fatigue, fevers, and respiratory problems. As her body weakened, Teresa faced one final journey, traveling to Alba de Tormes to establish a new convent. It was there, in a small, austere room in the convent, that Teresa would spend her final days.

Teresa died on October 4, 1582, at the age of 67. The exact timing of her death is significant because it occurred during the changeover from the Julian to the Gregorian calendar, which led to her death being recorded as both October 4 and October 15, 1582, depending on the calendar system. Her final words were said to have been, "My Lord, it is time to move on. Well then, may your will be done. O my Lord and my Spouse, the hour that I have longed for has come. It is time to meet one another."

These words reflect Teresa's lifelong devotion to God and her deep yearning for union with Him.

Teresa was buried in the convent at Alba de Tormes, and almost immediately, reports of miracles and healings attributed to her intercession began to circulate. Her reputation for holiness had already spread far and wide during her lifetime, but after her death, veneration of her grew rapidly. Her writings, particularly *The Interior Castle* and *The Way of Perfection*, gained widespread recognition for their spiritual depth and theological insight.

Teresa's canonization process began relatively soon after her death, propelled by the growing devotion to her and the miracles attributed to her intercession. On March 12, 1622, Teresa was canonized by Pope Gregory XV, alongside other notable saints, including St. Ignatius of Loyola, St. Francis Xavier, St. Philip Neri, and St. Isidore the Farmer. Teresa's canonization solidified her place as one of the greatest saints in the Catholic Church, and her life became a model of holiness, perseverance, and reform.

Continued Influence in the Church and Beyond

St. Teresa of Avila's influence extended far beyond her lifetime, continuing to shape Christian spirituality, mysticism, and monastic life for centuries. Her writings, which were initially composed for the nuns in her reformed Carmelite convents, have since become spiritual classics, studied and revered by people from all walks of life, including theologians, religious, and laypeople.

1. **Influence on Christian Mysticism and Spirituality**: Teresa's writings on prayer and mystical union with God have had a profound and lasting impact on the

55

development of Christian mysticism. Her clear, practical explanations of the stages of prayer and the soul's journey toward God have guided countless individuals in their own spiritual journeys. Teresa's teachings emphasize that the path to union with God is accessible to all people, not just mystics or religious. She demonstrated that through humility, perseverance, and trust in God's grace, anyone could experience a deep, personal relationship with the divine.

2. Teresa's works, particularly *The Interior Castle*, have influenced many subsequent spiritual writers and mystics, including her close collaborator St. John of the Cross, who shared her vision of contemplative prayer and spiritual ascent. Her approach to the interior life, with its focus on the gradual purification of the soul and union with God, continues to resonate with contemporary readers and spiritual seekers.

3. **Reform of Religious Life**: Teresa's reform of the Carmelite Order had a lasting impact on religious life within the Catholic Church. The Discalced Carmelites, with their emphasis on poverty, simplicity, and prayer, became a model for monastic reform throughout Europe. Teresa's reforms spread rapidly beyond Spain, with new Discalced Carmelite convents and monasteries being founded across the continent and eventually around the world.

4. Teresa's vision of religious life—focused on contemplative prayer, communal living, and self-surrender to God—has inspired generations of religious men and women. The Discalced Carmelite Order, which she founded, remains a vibrant and influential order within the Church, with thousands of members continuing to live out Teresa's

vision of radical devotion to God.

5. **Impact on Women in the Church**: As a woman who rose to prominence in the male-dominated world of the 16th-century Church, Teresa's life and work have had a lasting influence on the role of women in the Church. Teresa demonstrated that women could be spiritual leaders, reformers, and theological thinkers. Her writings, reforms, and mystical experiences earned her the respect of the highest Church authorities, including popes, kings, and bishops. In doing so, she broke down barriers for future generations of women in the Church.

6. Teresa's legacy as a woman of strength, intelligence, and deep spirituality has inspired many women in religious life and beyond to pursue their vocations with courage and determination. Her example continues to serve as a model for women seeking to play an active role in the spiritual renewal of the Church.

7. **Wider Cultural Influence**: Teresa's influence extends beyond the boundaries of the Church. Her life and writings have inspired artists, writers, and scholars across various disciplines. Her mystical experiences and teachings have been the subject of numerous works of art, literature, and theology. The famous sculpture *The Ecstasy of St. Teresa* by Gian Lorenzo Bernini, housed in the Church of Santa Maria della Vittoria in Rome, is one of the most iconic representations of her mystical experiences. Her life story has also inspired biographies, novels, and academic studies that explore her impact on theology, spirituality, and gender dynamics in the Church.

Legacy as a Doctor of the Church

One of the most significant moments in Teresa's posthumous legacy came in 1970 when she was declared a Doctor of the Church by Pope Paul VI. This honor, which has been bestowed on only a select few saints, recognizes Teresa's exceptional contributions to theology and spiritual teaching. Teresa was the first woman to be given this title, along with St. Catherine of Siena, who was named a Doctor of the Church on the same day.

The title of Doctor of the Church is reserved for saints whose writings and teachings are considered to have made a significant and enduring contribution to Christian theology. Teresa's works, particularly *The Interior Castle*, *The Way of Perfection*, and *The Life of Teresa of Jesus*, offer profound insights into the nature of prayer, the soul's relationship with God, and the process of spiritual transformation. Her teachings on the interior life and contemplative prayer have influenced countless people and have become essential reading for those seeking to deepen their spiritual lives.

In his declaration of Teresa as a Doctor of the Church, Pope Paul VI emphasized her importance as a theologian, mystic, and reformer, whose teachings have had a lasting impact on the Church. Teresa's recognition as a Doctor of the Church solidified her place among the greatest theological and spiritual minds in Christian history, and her works continue to be studied and revered by theologians, clergy, and laypeople alike.

Conclusion

St. Teresa of Avila's final years were marked by physical suffering, yet her dedication to the reform of the Carmelite Order and her deep relationship with God never wavered. Her death in 1582 was not the end of her influence; rather, it marked the beginning of her lasting legacy. Teresa's canonization in 1622, her continued influence on Christian mysticism and religious life, and her recognition as a Doctor of the Church have cemented her place as one of the most important figures in the history of the Catholic Church.

Teresa's writings on prayer, her reform of the Carmelite Order, and her mystical experiences have left an indelible mark on Christian spirituality. Her teachings on the interior life continue to guide spiritual seekers on their journey toward union with God, and her example of perseverance, humility, and love for God serves as a model for all who seek a deeper relationship with the divine.

Through her life, writings, and reforms, St. Teresa of Avila demonstrated that the path to holiness is open to all who are willing to dedicate themselves to God through prayer, self-denial, and trust in His grace. Her legacy as a reformer, mystic, and Doctor of the Church continues to inspire and guide the faithful, ensuring that her influence will endure for generations to come.

10

St. Teresa's Influence on Modern Spirituality

St. Teresa of Avila, though rooted in the spiritual and cultural context of 16th-century Spain, has had a profound and enduring influence on modern spirituality. Her teachings on prayer, her deep mystical experiences, and her reform of the Carmelite Order continue to resonate with people today, transcending time and cultural boundaries. Teresa's spirituality offers insights that remain relevant to contemporary Catholicism, has inspired a new understanding of feminine spirituality, and has fostered global devotion, making her one of the most universally venerated saints in the Christian tradition.

Impact on Contemporary Catholicism

St. Teresa of Avila's impact on contemporary Catholicism is profound, particularly in the areas of prayer, mysticism, and spiritual formation. Her teachings on the importance of contemplative prayer, the stages of spiritual development, and the soul's journey toward union with God have become essential components of Catholic spirituality. The continued study of her works, such as *The Interior Castle*, *The Way of Perfection*, and her autobiography, *The Life of Teresa of Jesus*, remains central to Catholic religious education, spiritual retreats, and individual spiritual development.

1. **Renewed Emphasis on Contemplative Prayer**: In an increasingly fast-paced world where distractions abound, Teresa's emphasis on contemplative prayer offers a much-needed path to spiritual stillness and inner peace. Her teaching that prayer is fundamentally about intimacy with God—rather than a mere recitation of words or formulas—has inspired many Catholics to seek deeper forms of prayer.

61

Teresa's exploration of the stages of prayer, from mental prayer to mystical union, provides contemporary believers with a practical roadmap for spiritual growth.

2. The Catholic Church's focus on contemplative prayer has seen a resurgence, particularly through initiatives like centering prayer and meditative practices, which reflect Teresa's emphasis on stillness, inner focus, and the deepening of one's relationship with God. Spiritual formation programs, Catholic retreats, and seminary education often incorporate Teresa's insights into the spiritual journey, showing her continued relevance for modern Catholics seeking a contemplative approach to faith.

3. **Influence on Religious Orders and Monastic Life**: Teresa's reforms of the Carmelite Order, emphasizing poverty, humility, and prayer, have had lasting effects on religious life within the Church. The Discalced Carmelites, founded by Teresa, continue to thrive and inspire both men and women who seek a life devoted to prayer and contemplation. The Carmelite charism of contemplative prayer, solitude, and devotion to God has influenced not only the Carmelites themselves but also other religious orders and lay movements that embrace contemplative spirituality.

4. Teresa's focus on the interior life has also resonated with modern Catholic religious orders that seek to combine an active life of ministry with a strong foundation of prayer and contemplation. Many religious communities today continue to look to Teresa as a model of balancing action with contemplation, an approach that emphasizes that the fruitfulness of one's work comes from one's relationship with God.

5. **Guidance for Personal Spiritual Growth**: In the personal

62

spiritual lives of Catholics, Teresa's writings offer practical advice and wisdom for deepening one's relationship with God. Her works remain widely read in spiritual direction and formation programs, where they help individuals navigate the challenges of prayer, discernment, and spiritual dryness. Teresa's honesty about her own struggles — her doubts, her spiritual dryness, and her persistence in prayer — makes her teachings accessible and relatable to modern Catholics who may face similar challenges.

6. Her insistence that spiritual growth requires perseverance, humility, and self-awareness continues to guide individuals in their pursuit of holiness. Teresa's writings encourage believers to trust in God's grace, even during times of difficulty, and to remain faithful to prayer even when consolations are absent. In this way, her influence on contemporary Catholicism lies not only in theological teachings but in the practical application of those teachings to everyday spiritual life.

Teresa's Role in Feminine Spirituality

St. Teresa of Avila is a pivotal figure in the development of feminine spirituality, both within the Catholic Church and in broader Christian traditions. As a female mystic, reformer, and Doctor of the Church, Teresa's life and writings have offered a powerful example of how women can engage in profound spiritual leadership, theological reflection, and mystical union with God. Her legacy has empowered women in the Church, influencing how feminine spirituality is understood and embraced today.

1. **A Model of Female Leadership**: Teresa's role as the

founder of the Discalced Carmelite Order and her successful navigation of the male-dominated Church hierarchy demonstrated that women could be influential spiritual leaders. Despite the limitations placed on women in the 16th century, Teresa's intelligence, determination, and sanctity earned her the respect of bishops, kings, and popes. Her ability to reform a major religious order and to influence Church doctrine and practice showed that women could exercise spiritual authority and leadership within the Catholic tradition.

2. Teresa's life continues to inspire modern women, especially those seeking to balance leadership with a deep commitment to prayer and humility. She is often seen as a role model for women who wish to engage in both contemplative spirituality and active service to the Church. Teresa's leadership style, which combined strong vision with deep humility, offers a model for modern women religious, theologians, and lay leaders seeking to influence the Church and society.

3. **Feminine Mysticism and Spirituality**: Teresa's writings reveal a uniquely feminine approach to mysticism, one that emphasizes the relational aspects of the soul's journey toward God. Her descriptions of the soul as a bride seeking union with her divine Spouse, and her use of maternal and intimate language to describe the soul's relationship with God, have resonated deeply with women throughout the centuries. Teresa's emphasis on the personal, emotional, and intimate dimensions of prayer has helped to shape how feminine spirituality is understood in both the Catholic Church and in broader Christian mysticism.

4. Many modern feminist theologians and spiritual writers

look to Teresa as a trailblazer who challenged traditional gender roles within the Church. Her writings, which frequently describe her own struggles with obedience, humility, and the limitations placed on her by her gender, offer a valuable perspective on the challenges women face in spiritual leadership. Teresa's legacy continues to inspire women to embrace their own unique spiritual gifts and to pursue a deeper relationship with God, regardless of societal or institutional barriers.

5. **Empowerment of Women in the Church**: St. Teresa's canonization as the first female Doctor of the Church in 1970, alongside St. Catherine of Siena, was a significant milestone in recognizing the contributions of women to Catholic theology and spirituality. Teresa's recognition as a Doctor of the Church affirmed that women could offer authoritative spiritual teachings that benefit the entire Church. Her example continues to empower women within the Church, particularly those who seek to engage in theological scholarship, spiritual direction, and leadership.

6. In modern times, Teresa's legacy has been embraced by Catholic women's movements, religious orders, and lay organizations that advocate for greater recognition of women's roles in the Church. Her life and writings have provided a theological foundation for understanding the unique contributions that women make to the spiritual and intellectual life of the Church. Teresa's influence on feminine spirituality has expanded beyond the Catholic Church, influencing Christian feminists and scholars across denominations who seek to recover the voices of women in Christian history.

65

Global Devotion to St. Teresa

St. Teresa of Avila's influence is not confined to Spain or Europe; she has become a global figure of devotion, with followers, devotees, and admirers from across the world. Her spiritual teachings, mysticism, and life of reform have made her one of the most beloved saints in Catholicism, inspiring people from all walks of life to seek a deeper relationship with God.

1. **The Spread of the Discalced Carmelites**: The global reach of Teresa's influence is most clearly seen in the spread of the Discalced Carmelite Order. After Teresa's death, her reform movement continued to expand across Europe, and by the 17th and 18th centuries, the Discalced Carmelites had established a presence in the Americas, Asia, and Africa. Today, the order has convents and monasteries in over 90 countries, making it one of the most widespread religious orders in the world.

2. The Discalced Carmelites, inspired by Teresa's vision of contemplative prayer and simplicity, continue to foster devotion to her and spread her teachings on prayer, humility, and union with God. The order's global presence ensures that Teresa's legacy is carried forward by a new generation of religious men and women, who continue to live out her spiritual vision in diverse cultural contexts.

3. **Devotion to St. Teresa in Popular Catholicism**: Beyond the religious orders, popular devotion to St. Teresa is widespread among Catholics around the world. Her feast day, celebrated on October 15, is observed with great reverence in many countries, particularly in Spain and Latin America, where she is considered one of the greatest saints of all time. Churches, schools, and religious institutions

across the globe bear her name, and her image is often found in Catholic homes, churches, and chapels.

4. Teresa's writings have been translated into numerous languages, making her spiritual wisdom accessible to people from all cultural backgrounds. In regions such as Latin America, where Carmelite spirituality has a strong presence, devotion to Teresa has taken on a distinctly local flavor, incorporating elements of the local culture while staying true to her emphasis on prayer and union with God.

5. **Influence on Interfaith Dialogue and Spirituality**: Teresa's mystical experiences and teachings on the inner life have also found resonance beyond the Catholic Church. Her works have been studied by scholars and spiritual seekers from other Christian denominations, as well as from non-Christian religious traditions. Teresa's emphasis on the interior journey toward God, her descriptions of mystical union, and her practical advice on prayer have made her a figure of interest in interfaith dialogues on spirituality and mysticism.

6. In recent years, Teresa's works have been incorporated into discussions on global spirituality, with her writings being compared to the teachings of mystics from other religious traditions, such as Sufism, Hinduism, and Buddhism. Teresa's insights into the nature of the soul's journey toward union with God have universal appeal, offering wisdom that transcends religious boundaries and speaks to the common human desire for spiritual fulfillment.

St. Teresa of Avila's influence on modern spirituality is vast and multifaceted. Her teachings on contemplative prayer, her role in reforming the Carmelite Order, and her example of feminine leadership have left an indelible mark on contemporary Catholicism and beyond. Teresa's works continue to inspire spiritual seekers around the world, guiding them on their journey toward union with God. Her legacy as a female mystic and reformer has empowered women within the Church and has provided a model for integrating deep spiritual contemplation with active leadership and reform.

Teresa's global devotion and her influence on interfaith dialogue further attest to her enduring impact, showing that her insights into the spiritual life resonate across cultures and religious traditions. As one of the Church's greatest saints and mystics, St. Teresa of Avila remains a guiding light for all those seeking a deeper, more intimate relationship with God, ensuring that her influence will continue to shape modern spirituality for generations to come.

11

Reflections on St. Teresa's Relevance Today

St. Teresa of Avila's teachings and spirituality continue to resonate with individuals and communities around the world, centuries after her death. Her insights into prayer, spiritual growth, and union with God remain deeply relevant to the challenges of modern life, offering guidance for those seeking inner peace, purpose, and connection with the divine. As a mystic, reformer, and teacher, Teresa's reflections on the soul's relationship with God provide a timeless roadmap for navigating the complexities of contemporary life, encouraging spiritual growth, resilience, and an abiding sense of inner peace.

Application of Her Teachings in Modern Life

In a world that is increasingly fast-paced and often distracted by materialism and technology, St. Teresa's teachings on prayer, contemplation, and detachment from worldly concerns offer a powerful antidote. Her emphasis on interior life, personal reflection, and union with God provides a path for those seeking meaning beyond the chaos of everyday life. Teresa's teachings remain as relevant today as they were in the 16th century because they speak to the universal human desire for connection, purpose, and spiritual fulfillment.

1. **The Need for Contemplative Prayer in a Busy World**: In to-day's world, where constant connectivity and information overload can leave individuals feeling anxious, distracted, and disconnected from themselves, Teresa's emphasis on contemplative prayer is particularly timely. Modern life often encourages multitasking, efficiency, and achievement, leaving little room for quiet reflection or deep communion with God. Teresa's approach to prayer—especially her

teachings on mental prayer and contemplation—invites individuals to step back from the busyness of life and enter into a place of stillness where they can encounter God directly.

2. Teresa understood that contemplative prayer is not an escape from the world, but rather a way to gain clarity, perspective, and strength to engage with life's challenges more fully. By cultivating an interior life through prayer, Teresa teaches that individuals can develop a deeper awareness of God's presence, which can bring greater peace and resilience in facing the demands of modern life. Her practice of retreating into silence, even while actively leading reforms, offers a model for balancing action with contemplation—something many people today strive for in their pursuit of work-life balance.

3. Today, practices like mindfulness, meditation, and centering prayer, often influenced by Teresa's teachings on contemplative prayer, have gained popularity as ways to manage stress, improve focus, and cultivate inner peace. Teresa's writings continue to provide invaluable resources for those seeking to incorporate contemplative practices into their daily routines, whether through traditional Christian prayer or more contemporary spiritual exercises.

4. **Detachment from Materialism and Consumer Culture**: Modern society often promotes material wealth, success, and the accumulation of possessions as measures of personal worth and happiness. St. Teresa's teachings on detachment offer a countercultural perspective that challenges these values. For Teresa, true happiness and peace are found not in material possessions or external achievements but in a deep relationship with God. She emphasized

that spiritual growth requires detachment from worldly concerns, not in a rejection of the world itself, but in a refusal to let material things dominate one's heart and mind.

5. Teresa's concept of detachment can be applied today by encouraging individuals to focus on what truly matters— relationships, spiritual development, and inner peace— rather than being consumed by the pursuit of material success. Her teachings call for a reevaluation of priorities, reminding people that while material possessions may provide temporary satisfaction, lasting fulfillment can only be found in a life oriented toward God.

6. In a consumer-driven society where people often find themselves caught in a cycle of wanting more and never feeling satisfied, Teresa's call to live simply and focus on God's will can be a liberating message. Her life of poverty, humility, and trust in God's providence offers a powerful example of how spiritual wealth far outweighs material wealth, and how the pursuit of God leads to true freedom and contentment.

7. **Spiritual Resilience in Times of Suffering and Uncertainty**: In an age where uncertainty, anxiety, and suffering—whether due to personal crises, global challenges, or health issues—can seem overwhelming, Teresa's reflections on the role of suffering in spiritual growth offer hope and encouragement. Throughout her life, Teresa experienced physical illness, spiritual trials, and opposition to her reforms, yet she found strength in her deep relationship with God. She teaches that suffering, when accepted with humility and trust in God, can be transformative and lead to greater spiritual maturity.

8. In *The Interior Castle*, Teresa describes how the soul's journey toward union with God often involves periods of darkness and difficulty, but she reassures her readers that these trials are necessary steps in the process of purification and growth. Her writings offer comfort to those who may feel lost or burdened by the challenges of life, reminding them that God is always present, even in moments of suffering.

9. For modern individuals facing personal struggles—whether related to health, loss, or existential uncertainty—Teresa's teachings on endurance, patience, and trust in God's providence provide a source of spiritual resilience. By following Teresa's example of surrendering one's will to God and trusting in His plan, individuals can find meaning and peace in the midst of suffering.

Her Guidance on Spiritual Growth and Inner Peace

St. Teresa's writings are deeply practical, offering step-by-step guidance for spiritual growth and the cultivation of inner peace. Her approach to prayer, self-awareness, and humility provides a clear framework for deepening one's relationship with God and achieving a state of inner harmony that transcends life's challenges. Teresa's teachings on the interior life continue to be a source of wisdom for anyone seeking to grow spiritually and find lasting peace.

1. **The Stages of Prayer and Spiritual Development**: One of Teresa's greatest contributions to Christian spirituality is her detailed explanation of the stages of prayer and spiritual growth, particularly as outlined in *The Interior Castle*. In this work, she describes the soul's journey

through seven mansions, each representing a deeper level of intimacy with God. Teresa's metaphor of the soul as a castle, with God dwelling in the innermost chamber, offers a powerful image for understanding the process of spiritual transformation.

2. Teresa teaches that spiritual growth is a gradual process that requires perseverance, humility, and a willingness to confront one's own weaknesses. She emphasizes that progress in prayer is not measured by extraordinary mystical experiences, but by an increasing alignment of one's will with God's will. In modern life, where quick fixes and immediate gratification are often valued, Teresa's emphasis on patience and persistence in the spiritual journey offers a countercultural message.

3. For those seeking to grow spiritually, Teresa's teachings provide a practical guide. She encourages her readers to begin with mental prayer and meditation, reflecting on God's love and presence in their lives. As they progress, individuals may experience deeper forms of prayer, such as contemplation, where the soul rests in God's presence without words or thoughts. Teresa's descriptions of these stages offer reassurance that spiritual dryness or difficulty in prayer is normal and part of the process of growth.

4. **Self-Knowledge and Humility**: Teresa's teachings on the importance of self-knowledge and humility are essential for anyone seeking spiritual growth and inner peace. She teaches that self-knowledge is the foundation of the spiritual life, as it allows individuals to recognize their weaknesses, limitations, and need for God's grace. Teresa emphasizes that humility is not about self-deprecation, but about seeing oneself as God sees us—with both our

strengths and our imperfections.

5. In modern life, where self-image is often shaped by social media, external validation, and the pressure to succeed, Teresa's emphasis on humility offers a refreshing perspective. She encourages individuals to let go of their need for approval and to focus instead on developing an honest relationship with themselves and with God. This process of self-awareness and humility leads to greater inner peace, as it frees individuals from the burden of constantly trying to prove themselves and allows them to rest in God's love.

6. **Union with God and Inner Peace**: The ultimate goal of Teresa's spiritual teachings is union with God, which she describes as the "spiritual marriage" between the soul and God. This state of union is characterized by profound inner peace, joy, and a sense of being fully united with God's will. For Teresa, true inner peace comes not from external circumstances, but from an interior relationship with God that transforms the soul from within.

7. In today's world, where many people struggle to find peace amidst the noise and stress of daily life, Teresa's teachings on union with God offer a path to lasting peace. She teaches that inner peace is not something that can be achieved through external success or control over one's environment, but through surrendering one's will to God and trusting in His love. By cultivating a life of prayer, humility, and detachment, individuals can experience the deep, abiding peace that comes from knowing they are loved by God and that their ultimate purpose is to be united with Him.

8. Teresa's message of inner peace is particularly relevant in a world marked by anxiety, conflict, and uncertainty.

Her teachings remind us that true peace is not found in the absence of challenges, but in the presence of God within us. By following her example of seeking God in the depths of our souls, we can find a peace that transcends the circumstances of life and offers lasting fulfillment.

St. Teresa of Avila's teachings continue to be deeply relevant in today's world, offering timeless wisdom for those seeking spiritual growth, inner peace, and a deeper relationship with God. Her practical guidance on prayer, self-knowledge, humility, and detachment provides a roadmap for navigating the complexities of modern life with grace and purpose. Teresa's reflections on suffering, perseverance, and trust in God's providence offer hope and encouragement to those facing personal challenges, while her teachings on contemplative prayer and union with God invite individuals to experience the profound peace that comes from an intimate relationship with the divine.

As one of the Church's greatest mystics and spiritual teachers, St. Teresa of Avila remains a guiding light for all those seeking to cultivate a life of prayer, reflection, and inner peace. Her relevance today is a testament to the enduring power of her insights, which continue to inspire and transform lives across the world. Through her example and her writings, Teresa invites us to journey inward, to seek God in the depths of our souls, and to discover the lasting peace that comes from union with Him.

12

Prayers and Devotions to St. Teresa of Avila

St. Teresa of Avila, known for her profound spirituality and mystical experiences, has become a source of inspiration and intercession for countless believers around the world. Her writings and teachings on prayer, contemplation, and spiritual growth offer valuable guidance for those seeking a deeper relationship with God. As a Doctor of the Church and a beloved saint, Teresa is also the subject of many prayers and devotions, through which the faithful ask for her intercession and follow her example in their spiritual lives. This chapter presents key prayers and devotions dedicated to St. Teresa of Avila, emphasizing their significance and the spiritual graces they seek.

Prayer for St. Teresa's Intercession

This prayer is commonly used by the faithful to seek the intercession of St. Teresa of Avila, especially for spiritual guidance, strength in adversity, and the deepening of one's prayer life.

Prayer for St. Teresa's Intercession

O most loving Lord Jesus, we come before you with hearts full of gratitude for the life and teachings of St. Teresa of Avila, your faithful servant and bride. Through her intercession, we ask that you grant us the grace to grow in love, humility, and perseverance in prayer. Like St. Teresa, may we seek you with all our hearts and surrender ourselves fully to your divine will. Help us to detach from the distractions of the world and to focus our lives on your presence within our souls.

We ask, O Lord, that through the intercession of St. Teresa, we may obtain the spiritual guidance and strength we need to endure the trials of this life and to grow in holiness. Grant us her courage in the face of difficulties, her wisdom in discerning your will, and her joy in experiencing union with you.

St. Teresa of Avila, pray for us, that we may be faithful in our pursuit of holiness and prayer. Lead us always to the heart of Christ, where we may find rest, peace, and eternal joy. Amen.

This prayer invites the faithful to connect with St. Teresa's spirituality and ask for her intercession, particularly for the grace to grow in prayer, humility, and perseverance in their spiritual journey.

Prayer of Self-Surrender to God (Inspired by St. Teresa)

St. Teresa of Avila was known for her deep trust in God's providence and her willingness to surrender completely to His will. This prayer is inspired by her writings, particularly her teachings on self-surrender and trust in God's perfect plan.

Prayer of Self-Surrender to God

Lord, grant me the grace to surrender myself completely to your will. Teach me, like St. Teresa, to trust in your divine providence and to abandon my own desires, fears, and anxieties into your loving hands. Let me not be troubled by the uncertainties of life, for I know that you hold all things in your care.

O my God, I place my entire life—my thoughts, my words, and my actions—at your feet. Lead me where you will, and help me to embrace whatever comes with joy and trust. Whether I face trials or blessings, suffering or peace, may I always see your hand guiding me toward the path of holiness.

St. Teresa of Avila, you who taught us to say, "Let nothing disturb you, let nothing frighten you, all things are passing, God never changes," intercede for me that I may live in this same peace and trust. Help me to surrender my life fully to Christ, knowing that in Him, I will find true freedom and joy. Amen.

This prayer encourages the faithful to embrace St. Teresa's spirit of complete trust in God, asking for the grace to surrender to His will and to find peace in the midst of life's uncertainties.

Novena to St. Teresa of Avila

A novena is a nine-day prayer, traditionally used to ask for a saint's intercession. The following novena to St. Teresa of Avila focuses on her virtues, her relationship with God, and the spiritual graces she offers through her intercession.

Day 1: St. Teresa's Humility

Lord, through the intercession of St. Teresa of Avila, grant me the grace of humility. May I learn to see myself as you see me, with both my weaknesses and my strengths, and rely entirely on your grace for everything. St. Teresa, teach me to be humble of heart, like you, and to seek God's will above all things. Amen.

Day 2: St. Teresa's Love for Prayer

St. Teresa, you who taught us the importance of mental prayer and contemplation, help me to grow in my prayer life. May I learn to quiet my mind and heart, so that I can listen to God's voice within. Help me to persevere in prayer, even when it is difficult, and to find joy in spending time with the Lord. Amen.

Day 3: St. Teresa's Trust in God

Lord, through the intercession of St. Teresa, help me to trust in you as she did. When I face uncertainty or fear, may I remember her words: "Let nothing disturb you; let nothing frighten you; God alone suffices." Give me the courage to trust in your plan for my life, even when I do not understand it. Amen.

Day 4: St. Teresa's Courage in Adversity

St. Teresa, you faced many trials in your life, but you never wavered in your faith. Help me to follow your example of courage and perseverance when I face difficulties. May I trust in God's strength to carry me through all challenges, and may I always remain faithful to Him. Amen.

Day 5: St. Teresa's Love for God

O St. Teresa, you loved God with your whole heart and desired nothing more than to be united with Him. Pray for me, that I may grow in my love for God each day. May I seek Him above all things and desire to be in His presence always. Amen.

Day 6: St. Teresa's Spirit of Detachment

Lord, through the intercession of St. Teresa, help me to let go of my attachment to worldly things. May I follow her example of detachment and live simply, focusing only on what truly matters— my relationship with you. Teach me to place my trust not in material possessions, but in your love and providence. Amen.

Day 7: St. Teresa's Patience in Suffering

O St. Teresa, you endured physical suffering and spiritual trials with patience and trust in God. Help me to bear my own sufferings with patience and offer them to God in union with Christ's suffering. May I never lose hope, knowing that God is always with me in my pain. Amen.

Day 8: St. Teresa's Love for the Church

St. Teresa, you worked tirelessly for the reform of the Church and the salvation of souls. Pray for me, that I may love the Church as you did and work for its renewal. May I be a faithful servant of Christ's Church and contribute to its mission of spreading the Gospel. Amen.

Day 9: St. Teresa's Desire for Union with God

Lord, through the intercession of St. Teresa, grant me the grace of desiring union with you above all things. Help me to seek you with all my heart, mind, and soul, and to let go of anything that keeps me from you. May I one day experience the perfect union with you that St. Teresa so longed for in her life. Amen.

The novena to St. Teresa allows the faithful to reflect on her virtues and seek her intercession over nine days, asking for the grace to grow in humility, prayer, trust, and love for God.

Litany of St. Teresa of Avila

A litany is a form of prayer involving a series of petitions, followed by invocations asking for a saint's intercession. The following litany invokes St. Teresa's virtues and requests her help in various aspects of the spiritual life.

Litany of St. Teresa of Avila

Lord, have mercy on us.

Christ, have mercy on us.

Lord, have mercy on us.

Christ, hear us.

Christ, graciously hear us.

God, the Father of Heaven,

Have mercy on us.

God the Son, Redeemer of the world,

Have mercy on us.

God the Holy Spirit,

Have mercy on us.

Holy Trinity, one God,

Have mercy on us.

Holy Mary, Mother of God,

Pray for us.

St. Joseph, Patron of the Carmelite Order,

Pray for us.

St. Teresa of Avila, Doctor of the Church,

Pray for us.

St. Teresa, devoted servant of God,

Pray for us.

St. Teresa, lover of prayer and contemplation,

Pray for us.

St. Teresa, reformer of religious life,

Pray for us.

St. Teresa, tireless worker for the Church,

Pray for us.
St. Teresa, model of humility and trust in God,
Pray for us.
St. Teresa, patient in suffering and trial,
Pray for us.
St. Teresa, teacher of the interior life,
Pray for us.
St. Teresa, who taught the way of perfection,
Pray for us.
St. Teresa, who sought union with God above all,
Pray for us.
Lamb of God, who takes away the sins of the world,
Spare us, O Lord.
Lamb of God, who takes away the sins of the world,
Graciously hear us, O Lord.
Lamb of God, who takes away the sins of the world,
Have mercy on us.
Let us pray.

O God, who through St. Teresa of Avila did inspire many to seek perfection through prayer and contemplation, grant that through her intercession we may always be devoted to a life of holiness and union with you. Help us to grow in humility, patience, and love, as we follow her example of trust and surrender to your divine will. We ask this through Christ our Lord. Amen.

This litany invokes St. Teresa's virtues and requests her intercession in key areas of spiritual life, helping the faithful draw closer to God through her guidance.

St. Teresa of Avila's prayers and devotions offer powerful means for the faithful to seek her intercession and follow her path of holiness. Her teachings on prayer, trust in God, and detachment from worldly concerns provide timeless wisdom for deepening one's spiritual life. Through novenas, litanies, and personal prayers inspired by St. Teresa's example, believers can grow in their relationship with God, find strength in times of trial, and pursue a life of union with the divine, just as St. Teresa did in her own journey toward holiness.

13

The Timeless Spirit of St. Teresa of Avila

The life, teachings, and legacy of St. Teresa of Avila have transcended the boundaries of time, geography, and culture. Her spirit, forged in the fires of mystical prayer, reform, and personal suffering, continues to inspire and guide those seeking a deeper relationship with God. From her early days as a young Carmelite nun to her final years as a tireless reformer and mystic, Teresa's journey was one of transformation, marked by her singular focus on union with God. Today, the timeless spirit of St. Teresa lives on, resonating with individuals who long for spiritual depth, inner peace, and a life rooted in prayer.

A Life of Transformation and Trust

St. Teresa of Avila's life can be seen as a constant journey of transformation—a pilgrimage toward spiritual maturity and intimacy with God. Born into a noble Spanish family, Teresa initially struggled with the distractions of worldly life, but over time, she grew into one of the greatest spiritual leaders in Christian history. Her personal evolution from a Carmelite nun grappling with spiritual dryness to a reformer and Doctor of the Church is a testament to the transformative power of prayer and God's grace.

Teresa's trust in God, particularly in the face of physical illness, internal doubt, and opposition to her reforms, is one of the most compelling aspects of her legacy. She taught that suffering and trials are necessary for the purification of the soul and should be embraced as part of the spiritual journey. This message is as relevant today as it was in the 16th century. Modern life is filled with its own unique challenges—mental health struggles, social and political uncertainties, and personal crises—but Teresa's example reminds us that through faith and trust in God, we can find peace, resilience, and a sense of purpose.

Her ability to trust God, even when His presence felt distant, offers hope to those who experience spiritual dryness or the "dark night of the soul." Teresa understood that the soul's journey toward God involves moments of darkness and uncertainty, but she reassures us that these moments are necessary steps toward a deeper, more authentic union with the divine.

The Relevance of Her Teachings Today

The timeless spirit of St. Teresa of Avila is most evident in her teachings on prayer, humility, and spiritual growth, which continue to offer guidance for those navigating the complexities of modern life. In an age where many people are searching for meaning, peace, and fulfillment in the midst of constant distractions, Teresa's call to an interior life of contemplation and union with God remains deeply relevant.

1. **The Call to Contemplative Prayer**: Teresa's emphasis on contemplative prayer offers a pathway to inner peace and spiritual growth in a world dominated by materialism and noise. Her teachings on mental prayer—especially her advice to simply "be" with God in silence—are particularly resonant today. Many people feel overwhelmed by the demands of modern life, but Teresa invites us to carve out moments of stillness in which we can connect with God and nurture our inner life.

2. In *The Interior Castle*, Teresa guides us through the stages of prayer, reminding us that each soul is a "castle" where God dwells. This profound metaphor invites us to enter into our own interior world, to explore the different "mansions" of the soul, and to grow closer to God in the process. In

a world that often prioritizes external achievement over internal depth, Teresa's message is a refreshing reminder of the power of introspection and spiritual contemplation.

3. **The Power of Humility and Self-Knowledge**: Teresa's teachings on humility and self-knowledge are equally timeless. She insisted that true spiritual growth requires a deep awareness of our weaknesses, limitations, and need for God's grace. For Teresa, humility is the foundation of the spiritual life—it is only by recognizing our own inadequacies that we can fully open ourselves to God's transformative power.

4. In a society that often values self-promotion, success, and external validation, Teresa's call to humility is a counter-cultural message. She teaches us that true greatness lies not in outward accomplishments, but in our willingness to surrender to God's will and allow Him to work through us. Her writings encourage us to let go of pride, ego, and the need for control, and instead to embrace a life of radical dependence on God's grace.

5. **Endurance and Perseverance in Faith**: One of the most striking aspects of Teresa's legacy is her emphasis on perseverance in prayer and faith, even in the face of difficulty. Throughout her life, Teresa experienced physical illness, spiritual desolation, and opposition to her reform efforts, yet she remained unwavering in her commitment to God. She often wrote about the challenges of maintaining a prayer life, especially during times of spiritual dryness, but she always encouraged perseverance, trusting that God would reward faithfulness.

6. Teresa's example of endurance is particularly inspiring for those today who may feel discouraged in their spiritual

88

journey. She reminds us that the path to union with God is not easy, but it is worth the struggle. Her teachings provide hope and encouragement for anyone who feels lost or weary in their faith, offering the assurance that God is always present, even when He seems distant.

Teresa's Enduring Legacy in the Church and Beyond

Teresa's influence extends far beyond the walls of Carmelite convents or even the boundaries of the Catholic Church. Her teachings and spirituality have been embraced by people of all faiths and backgrounds, making her one of the most universally revered saints in Christian history. Her legacy as a reformer, mystic, and spiritual teacher continues to shape Christian theology and practice, and her writings remain essential reading for anyone seeking to grow in prayer and holiness.

1. **Doctor of the Church and Global Devotion**: Teresa's recognition as a Doctor of the Church affirms the theological depth and spiritual wisdom of her writings. Her works, particularly *The Interior Castle* and *The Way of Perfection*, have been studied and revered by generations of theologians, scholars, and spiritual seekers. The Discalced Carmelite Order, which she reformed and revitalized, continues to thrive across the globe, with thousands of nuns, monks, and laypeople carrying forward her vision of contemplative prayer and simplicity.

2. Devotion to St. Teresa has grown far beyond Spain, where she lived and worked. Today, she is venerated around the world, particularly in countries with a strong Carmelite presence, such as Italy, France, Latin America, and the Philippines. Her feast day, celebrated on October 15,

is marked by special Masses, prayers, and devotions in churches and communities across the globe, and her spiritual wisdom continues to inspire both clergy and laypeople alike.

3. **A Model of Feminine Spirituality and Leadership**: As a female reformer and spiritual leader in the 16th century, Teresa's life and work have had a lasting impact on how the Church views the role of women in religious life. Her ability to navigate the challenges of her time, combined with her deep mystical experiences and theological insights, has made her a model of feminine spirituality and leadership. She has empowered generations of women in the Church to pursue their vocations with courage, conviction, and humility.

4. Teresa's influence on feminine spirituality is particularly evident in her writings, which emphasize the relational aspects of the soul's journey toward God. Her use of intimate language to describe the soul's union with God has resonated deeply with women throughout the centuries, offering a powerful example of how women can engage with theology and spirituality in a way that is both personal and profound.

The Spirit of St. Teresa in Modern Spirituality

The spirit of St. Teresa of Avila continues to breathe life into modern spirituality, offering a path for those seeking to reconcile their inner lives with the demands of the world. Whether through her teachings on prayer, her call to trust in God's providence, or her example of humility and perseverance, Teresa's message is one of hope, transformation, and divine intimacy.

1. **A Bridge Between Action and Contemplation**: Teresa's life was a balance of action and contemplation. As a reformer, she was deeply involved in the practical work of founding convents, navigating ecclesiastical politics, and leading her fellow nuns. Yet, at the same time, she remained rooted in a life of prayer and contemplation, constantly seeking union with God. This balance between action and contemplation is a model for modern life, where individuals often struggle to find harmony between their spiritual aspirations and the demands of daily living.

2. Teresa's example shows us that it is possible to live a life of deep spiritual devotion while still engaging with the world. Her ability to integrate her interior life with her external responsibilities serves as an inspiration for those who seek to bring their faith into every aspect of their lives, whether in work, family, or community.

3. **A Call to Seek God in All Things**: Ultimately, the timeless spirit of St. Teresa of Avila is a call to seek God in all things. Whether through prayer, work, suffering, or joy, Teresa teaches that God is present in every moment of our lives, inviting us into a deeper relationship with Him. Her life and teachings remind us that the spiritual journey is not about escaping the world, but about finding God within it—within our hearts, our relationships, and our daily experiences.

4. In an age where many people feel disconnected from their spiritual roots, Teresa's message is a powerful reminder that God is always with us, waiting for us to turn to Him in prayer. Her writings invite us to explore the depths of our souls, to trust in God's plan, and to experience the profound peace that comes from union with the divine.

St. Teresa of Avila's spirit is as alive today as it was during her lifetime, continuing to inspire, guide, and challenge those who seek a deeper relationship with God. Her teachings on prayer, humility, and perseverance remain timeless, offering a pathway to inner peace and spiritual growth in the midst of modern life's complexities. As a Doctor of the Church, mystic, and reformer, Teresa's legacy endures in the hearts of believers around the world, reminding us that the journey toward God is one of continual transformation, trust, and love. Through her example, we are invited to follow her path of prayer, trust in God's providence, and seek the divine presence that dwells within each of us. In this way, the timeless spirit of St. Teresa of Avila continues to lead us toward union with God, the ultimate goal of every soul's journey.

14

Conclusion

St. Teresa of Avila's legacy is one of profound spiritual wisdom, mystical insight, and practical reform. Born into a complex and turbulent period of religious change in the 16th century, she navigated personal struggles, societal limitations, and ecclesiastical opposition to become one of the most revered figures in Christian spirituality. As a reformer, mystic, writer, and Doctor of the Church, Teresa's contributions have shaped Christian thought and devotion for centuries, and her relevance continues to extend far beyond her lifetime.

Teresa's Spiritual Depth and Mysticism

At the heart of St. Teresa's spiritual legacy is her deep commitment to prayer and contemplation. Her teachings on prayer, especially her development of mental and contemplative prayer, have had an unparalleled influence on Christian mysticism. Teresa's *Interior Castle* remains one of the most celebrated works in spiritual literature, offering a systematic and insightful roadmap for the soul's journey toward union with God. Through her descriptions of the seven mansions, Teresa illustrates the progressive deepening of the soul's intimacy with God, culminating in spiritual marriage—a metaphor for complete union with the divine.

What sets Teresa apart from many other mystics is her ability to articulate her profound experiences in a way that is both relatable and accessible. She provides practical guidance, acknowledging the difficulties of prayer, spiritual dryness, and distractions, which makes her advice deeply applicable to the everyday spiritual struggles of believers. Her teachings emphasize that prayer is not an exercise in perfect focus or eloquence, but rather a loving encounter with God that demands perseverance and humility.

Her writings encourage Christians to embark on an inward journey, where they can discover the presence of God within themselves. In a world that often prioritizes external achievements and material success, Teresa's message of turning inward to find true peace and meaning resonates strongly. Her emphasis on self-knowledge, humility, and detachment from worldly concerns offers a countercultural approach to spiritual fulfillment, rooted in a deep relationship with God.

Reforming the Carmelite Order and the Church

St. Teresa's impact extends beyond her mystical writings—she was also a significant reformer who reshaped the Carmelite Order and contributed to the broader Counter-Reformation efforts within the Catholic Church. Her tireless work to establish the Discalced Carmelites, a branch of the order that adhered more strictly to the original ideals of poverty, simplicity, and prayer, exemplified her commitment to spiritual renewal. Teresa's reforms were not merely structural; they were deeply spiritual, aimed at restoring the heart of religious life to its foundation in prayer and contemplation.

The success of her reforms, particularly in collaboration with

St. John of the Cross, demonstrated Teresa's leadership and vision. Despite facing considerable resistance from within the Carmelite Order and the Church hierarchy, she persevered, motivated by her desire to bring the order back to its spiritual roots. Her work led to the establishment of numerous reformed Carmelite convents and monasteries, many of which became centers of prayer and spiritual renewal during a time of great religious upheaval.

Teresa's reforms had a lasting impact on monastic life, influencing not only the Carmelite Order but also other religious orders that sought to renew their spiritual practices. Her vision of a life centered on prayer, humility, and detachment from material wealth continues to inspire those in religious life today. Moreover, her role in the Counter-Reformation was a powerful testament to the Catholic Church's capacity for internal reform and spiritual revitalization in response to the challenges of the Protestant Reformation.

A Pioneer of Feminine Spirituality and Leadership

St. Teresa of Avila's significance is further enhanced by her role as a pioneering female figure in the Church. Living in an era when women had limited opportunities for leadership within the Church, Teresa not only defied these constraints but became a powerful and respected voice in spiritual matters. Her leadership in reforming the Carmelite Order and her mystical writings challenged traditional gender roles, demonstrating that women could contribute meaningfully to theological and spiritual discourse.

Teresa's recognition as a Doctor of the Church in 1970 was a groundbreaking moment in the history of the Catholic Church. Alongside St. Catherine of Siena, she became one of the first women to receive this title, affirming her authority as a spiritual teacher and theologian. Her elevation to this status is a testament to the depth of her spiritual and theological insights, which continue to shape Christian spirituality and mysticism today.

Her writings, particularly on the interior life and the soul's journey toward God, reflect a uniquely feminine approach to mysticism, emphasizing relational aspects of prayer and union with God. Teresa's use of intimate, loving language to describe the soul's relationship with God has resonated deeply with women throughout the centuries, making her a symbol of feminine spiritual empowerment. Her courage, intelligence, and sanctity continue to inspire women in the Church, encouraging them to pursue their vocations with confidence and humility.

Relevance in Modern Spirituality

St. Teresa's teachings remain deeply relevant to contemporary spirituality, offering guidance for those seeking to navigate the challenges of modern life. In an era marked by distractions, materialism, and superficial success, Teresa's call to contemplative prayer and interior reflection provides a much-needed reminder of the importance of the inner life. Her writings invite people to slow down, turn inward, and cultivate a relationship with God that brings peace, meaning, and fulfillment.

Her emphasis on perseverance in prayer, especially during times of spiritual dryness or desolation, speaks to the experience of many modern Christians who may struggle with faith in a secularized world. Teresa's honesty about her own difficulties in prayer and her unwavering trust in God's providence offers encouragement to those facing similar struggles today. She teaches that the spiritual journey is not without challenges, but that true intimacy with God is worth every effort.

Moreover, Teresa's teachings on detachment from worldly

concerns resonate strongly in a world where consumerism and the pursuit of success often dominate. Her insistence that true happiness comes from a life focused on God, rather than on material possessions or external achievements, offers a countercultural message of spiritual freedom. Teresa's legacy encourages modern believers to seek fulfillment not in the things of this world, but in the presence of God, who alone can satisfy the deepest longings of the human soul.

Conclusion: The Timeless Spirit of St. Teresa of Avila

The legacy of St. Teresa of Avila is one of spiritual depth, resilience, and reform. Her writings continue to guide those seeking a deeper relationship with God, her reforms have left an indelible mark on religious life, and her role as a spiritual leader and mystic has inspired countless generations. As a Doctor of the Church, her theological and spiritual insights remain a cornerstone of Christian mysticism, influencing both scholars and everyday believers.

St. Teresa's journey toward union with God, marked by prayer, humility, and perseverance, serves as a model for all who seek to grow in holiness. Her life of reform and leadership, despite opposition and personal struggles, is a powerful testament to the strength that comes from unwavering faith and trust in God. Whether through her teachings on contemplative prayer, her leadership in the reform of the Carmelite Order, or her role as a pioneer of feminine spirituality, St. Teresa of Avila continues to inspire a path of holiness and love that transcends time.

Her spirit endures as a beacon of light for those on their own spiritual journeys, inviting all to enter the interior castle of their souls, where God awaits. Through her life, writings, and the lasting impact of her reforms, St. Teresa of Avila remains a timeless figure in the Church, a guide for all who seek union with the divine.

Printed in Dunstable, United Kingdom